The 80/20 Revolution

Why the creative individual—not the corporation or capital—is king

The 80/20 Revolution

How you can create and capture wealth and wellbeing

Richard Koch

NICHOLAS BREALEY
PUBLISHING

LONDON

To Matthew

First published by
Nicholas Brealey Publishing in 2002

3–5 Spafield Street
Clerkenwell, London
EC1R 4QB, UK
Tel: +44 (0)20 7239 0360
Fax: +44 (0)20 7239 0370

PO Box 700
Yarmouth
Maine 04096, USA
Tel: (888) BREALEY
Fax: (207) 846 5181

http://www.nbrealey-books.com
www.the8020principle.com

ISBN 1-85788-305-5

British Library Cataloguing in Publication Data
A catalogue record for this book is available from the
British Library.

Printed in Finland by WS Bookwell.

Contents

Part I: The Rise of 80/20 People   **1**

1   Introduction to the 80/20 revolution   2
2   The rise of the creative individual   14

Part II: The Nine Essentials of 80/20 Success   **33**

3   Enlist your most creative 20 percent   35
4   Enlist and mutate great ideas   50
5   Enlist the vital few profit forces   69
6   Enlist Einstein   86
7   Enlist great individuals   97
8   Enlist your firm   117
9   Enlist other firms   141
10   Enlist capital   157
11   Enlist zigzag progress   172

Part III: The 80/20 Revolution   **183**

12   From capitalism to individualism   184
13   What if?   200

Appendix: The roots and ramifications of the revolution   217
Index   237
Acknowledgments   242

Part I

The Rise of 80/20 People

1 *Introduction to*

"As business changes, the individual is the one who brings tools to the company."

Philip Harris, CEO, PJM Interconnection

"It's almost as though the village blacksmiths of the world can now build axles in their backyards, and assemble them together and compete with General Motors. And that's literally what is going on. We have proof through the Linux operating system."

Paul Maritz, vice-president, Microsoft

"In all of these industries, the key unit of value creation is the individual ... the logic of deconstructing value chains is carried to its limit: individual employees (the smallest possible sliver of the business) extract the value that they uniquely create."

Philip Evans and Thomas S. Wurster, Boston Consulting Group

"Take away our twenty most important people, and I tell you we would become an unimportant company."

Bill Gates, chairman, Microsoft

"The emperor of the future will be the emperor of ideas."

Winston Churchill

"If nature has made any one thing less susceptible than all others of exclusive property, it is the action of the thinking power called an idea."

Thomas Jefferson

the 80/20 Revolution

❖ **There is a new way to create wealth** that is better than the traditional route of managerial capitalism.

❖ **Creative individuals** are at the heart of the new revolution. Creative individuals are more important to wealth generation than are corporations or capital. Individualism is replacing capitalism.

❖ **The revolution follows one simple principle**—the 80/20 principle. Success comes from an exclusive focus on the few very powerful forces operating in an arena. The most important forces to which the 80/20 principle applies are ideas and individuals. The principle also applies to all the other raw materials of enterprise: customers, partners, technologies, products, suppliers, and capital.

❖ **Wealth is most effectively multiplied** by subtraction and rearrangement of industries, not through the traditional routes of aggregation of activities and assets. More separate enterprises are created, spawned by a new idea from new individuals, and linked together by markets rather than by hierarchy and central planning.

❖ **The 80/20 revolution is as important** as the three other transitions in economic history: the agricultural revolution, the industrial revolution, and the managerial revolution. These resulted in quite different economies and societies. The same will probably happen again, over the next two decades.

❖ **Perhaps the most seminal change has already happened**—the most successful corporations now revolve around a few individuals. The corporation serves the individuals, not the other way round. Yet this does not apply universally. Most of the economy—although not the most profitable part—still follows the old pattern of managerial capitalism. When this ceases to be true, the economy will change abruptly and radically. We will witness a huge transfer of wealth to individuals and away from institutions, to entrepreneurs and away from passive investors.

❖ **Individuals who want to benefit** by being part of the 80/20 revolution can do so by taking some straightforward steps. These are fully described in Part II.

This book is about a revolution that is changing the lives of individuals, just as the individuals themselves are changing the world. I call the revolutionaries "80/20 people"—individuals and small teams who can use the 80/20 principle to create wealth and wellbeing. You may already be an 80/20 person without knowing it, but if you are not, you have everything to gain by becoming one.

A brief history of the 80/20 Principle

In 1897, Italian economist Vilfredo Pareto (1848–1923) discovered a regular pattern in distributions of wealth or income, no matter the country or time period concerned. The distribution was extremely skewed toward the top end: A small minority of the top earners always accounted for a large majority of the total. Pareto was eventually able to predict the results accurately before looking at the data.

Pareto was greatly excited by his discovery, which he rightly believed was of enormous importance not just to economics but to society as well. But he managed only to enthuse a few fellow economists. Although he could write lucidly on less momentous subjects, his exposition of the

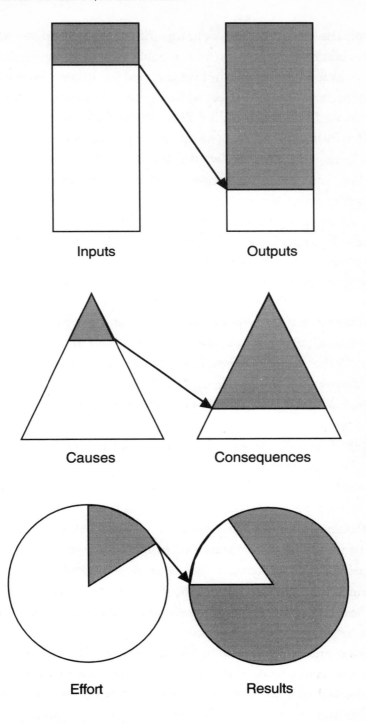

Inputs   Outputs

Causes   Consequences

Effort   Results

Figure 1 The 80/20 Principle

"Pareto principle" lay buried beneath windy academic language and dense algebraic formulae.

Pareto's idea only began to become widely known when Joseph Moses Juran, one of the two great quality gurus of the twentieth century, renamed it the "Rule of the Vital Few." In his 1951 tome *The Quality Control Handbook*, which became hugely influential in Japan and later in the West, Juran contrasted the "vital few" to the "trivial many," showing how quality faults could be largely eliminated, cheaply and quickly, by focusing on the vital few causes.[1] Juran, who went to live in Japan in 1954, taught executives there to improve quality and features at the same time as copying from the US. Between 1957 and 1989 Japan grew faster than any other industrial economy.

In the US and Europe in the 1960s, the Pareto principle became widely known as the "80/20 rule" or "80/20 principle." While it was not wholly accurate, this description was snappy and influential. Engineers and computer experts began to use the principle routinely.

The 80/20 principle observes that 80 percent of results flow from 20 percent of causes. It is an empirical "law" that has been verified in economics, business, and interdisciplinary science. Thus most of what exists in the universe—what we do, and all other forces, resources, and ideas—is of little value and has little result; yet a few things work fantastically well and have tremendous impact. There is no magic in the 80 and the 20, which are merely approximations. The point is that the world is not 50/50. Effort and reward are not linearly related. The universe is wonky.

Most of the universe is meaningless noise, yet a few forces are fantastically powerful and productive. Isolate those powerful, creative forces, within and around us, and, hey presto, we can exert incredible influence.

In 1963, IBM spotted that about 80 percent of a computer's time is spent executing less than 20 percent of its operating code. The IBM engineers rewrote the code to make the key 20 percent much more accessible and user-friendly, thereby securing market leadership. The software advances of the last 30 years—from Lotus to Microsoft to Linux—have taken this idea very much further.

In 1997 I wrote *The 80/20 Principle*,[2] the first book on the subject. I showed how the principle could be applied not merely to help corporations drive business results, but also to help individuals improve their lives. To become effective or happy, realize the importance of just a few people or things. If you concentrate on the few things that work best for you, you can get what you want. You can multiply your effectiveness, and even your happiness. This was new ground, since nobody had previously linked the principle to individual fulfillment.

I struck a chord. As many readers around the world attested, the 80/20 principle is a fantastically useful way to get more out of life.

This new book, however, has a very different theme. *The 80/20 Principle* showed how companies could use the principle to drive business results and how individuals could improve their personal lives—but not their professional lives. *The 80/20 Revolution* makes the link between the 80/20 principle and the rise of individuals, which has never been made before. It explains how the world is changing and demonstrates that the 80/20 principle is a liberating and amazingly powerful, practical tool for individuals to create great new things.

Value comes from growth

The most interesting and valuable part of business is not the maintenance of existing operations: doing efficiently today what we did yesterday, how we did it yesterday. Organizations are great at maintaining the status quo, but if this was all we did, the economy would never grow.

Growth is more important. Growth means creating something new and valuable. Growth is ultimately driven by individuals and small, self-selected teams of individuals, operating both within established corporations and in new ventures.

The most formidable weapon for growth in business is the 80/20 principle, creatively applied by individuals and small teams of individuals. With the 80/20 principle, individuals can leverage the most powerful forces around them—tangible, but especially intangible ones—to dazzle the world and provide customers with much more of what they want for much less of what they wish to conserve (money, resources, time, space, and energy).

80/20 people in organizations

Individuals are usually only partly aware of what they could do to create wealth and wellbeing. They may also be unaware of what they are already doing. In this book you will encounter several people who are creating enormous wealth for others, but who do not realize it. They are already 80/20 people, although they are not yet reaping the rewards appropriate to their creativity. They think they are cogs in a corporate machine, while in reality they are at the heart of wealth creation and economic growth.

Even if you work for a large or prestigious organization, if you create something new that reflects your individuality and your ideas, then *you* are the primary wealth creator. Usually, however, your corporation keeps most of the wealth that you create. Once you realize the disparity, you can narrow the gap. Whether you leave the firm or stay within it, you should be in control.

Those who can create wealth—and know that they can—are able to dictate their own terms. Money is important, yet what most people want is not wealth but happiness. Wealth is a means to happiness, but it is not the main one. What most people want is control over their lives. They want the ability to choose how they live: what work they do, how they interact with friends and colleagues, the quality of their personal relationships, how they make things better for other people, and how they think about themselves.

What you gain as an 80/20 individual is the right to control your life: your work life, your personal life, and the intervening spaces where they collide or mesh, inducing despair or triumph. For example, you may be able to strike a completely different deal with your current employer. There is a whole range of new mechanisms enabling 80/20 people to be "half in and half out," retaining contact and continuity with colleagues while also having real ownership in a new venture. For many 80/20 people these hybrid mechanisms are greatly superior to the traditional alternatives, either staying put and being exploited as an employee, or starting a new business from scratch.

My premise is simple—if you add great value, know you add great value, and can demonstrate that you add great value, you can reasonably insist on setting the agenda and the context in which you provide it. You can set your own material and nonmaterial rewards because, whatever you choose to take, it is less than you give. If this simple view upsets existing arrangements, so much the worse for them. You create—you are in control.

The 80/20 principle is at the heart of creation

People think that creativity is a largely a matter of talent, or experience, or luck. They are wrong. Talent, experience, and luck are all key elements. But there is something more fundamental, something wonderfully accessible and powerful, that you can use to multiply your creative effect.

The 80/20 principle is central to all acts of creation. In business it is behind any innovation, any extra value. It is the entrepreneurial principle, the formula for value creation, not just for entrepreneurs but for managers and organizations generally.

A few powerful forces lie behind any act of creation. Take plant growth, the most efficient source of food, and therefore life, throughout the ages. What makes plants grow? Rain is clearly important. And what causes rain? Clouds—but a few clouds create most rain. They create it at particular times, in particular locations. Fertile land is also important. Land fertility is partly a matter of rain, but there are other influences, for example the variety and number of plants and animals that have used the land before. A few pieces of land are very much more fertile than others—not a little better, not even twice or three times as good, but tens of times better. A few influences are always critical, and a few inputs always lead to a large majority of results.

Creation can either be unconscious, as with clouds, or conscious, as with humankind. Our history, especially that of the past three centuries, demonstrates that people can multiply the effectiveness of the rest of nature many times over—hundreds, thousands, even millions of times. (We can also apply similar multiples to nature's destructive forces, but let's pass on that for the moment.) There have been three great human inventions that have driven the number of people on our planet, and our living standards, into the stratosphere.

One was the invention of agriculture some 9,000 years ago. Before that, our ancestors gathered wild plants and fruits and hunted wild animals. Deliberate cultivation of plants and breeding of animals for food dramatically increased the size and complexity of human society.

The second breakthrough was the agricultural revolution of the eighteenth and nineteenth centuries, the mechanization of agriculture and the application of industrial techniques. Whereas 300 years ago the vast majority of the population worked the land to make a bare living from it, today in the developed world the same proportion do *not* work on the land. Yet agricultural production has increased thousands of times, supporting a vastly greater population with more and better food.

The third breakthrough has been the industrial revolution, the alliance between science and business that defines the modern world.

How can such extraordinary conscious acts of creation happen? We could describe them in many different ways, but there are three characteristics of any conscious creation.

One is that **creation is a matter of rearranging things that already exist.** "There is nothing new under the sun," as the Preacher said in the Old Testament.[3] The invention of agriculture around 7,000 BC involved taking what already existed in nature and rearranging it to make it dramatically more productive. The agricultural revolution after 1750 rearranged the ancient elements of production, applying the leverage of scale and machinery. Biotechnology today imitates what nature does, speeds it up, and applies new permutations. Sand has been around for ever, abundant and of little or no value; yet a microchip, made of silica, formed from sand, can be extremely valuable.[4]

The second common characteristic of conscious creation is that **it leverages the most powerful forces available.** There are countless natural forces, both of species and inanimate forces (such as clouds). Only a few of them are really useful for creation. And within each species or type of force, a small minority are much more powerful and useful than the rest. Among all plants, a few vegetables are the most nutritious. Among farming methods, a few are pre-eminent. Among all areas of production, a few are the most fertile.

Breakthroughs in productivity occur when the most productive way of doing something is further leveraged by scale, capital, or a particular technique. Breakthroughs spring from thought and experimentation. The most powerful force that thought can leverage is thought itself. Great things are created when new ideas leverage not only the most powerful physical forces, but also the most powerful ideas.

Hence the third and most intriguing aspect of conscious creation: *Creation occurs when ideas and individuals collide and collude*. Of course, the raw materials of creation are physical, the stuff the universe makes available to us. But the essence of creation is not physical, it is intellectual.

The idea for the microchip did not arise from playing around with sand in the desert, but from playing around with other related ideas. Creation requires ideas and individuals, usually a few of each—and not too many. All great scientific breakthroughs can be traced to a few fertile ideas that are pondered and rearranged by an individual or a small team. All business growth arises in the same way. Doing something differently, creating something new—all such actions start with an idea. The idea normally originates with an individual, and is refined within a small team.

Business creation has a fourth common characteristic: If it is to survive, even for a time, *a business innovation has to improve value to customers*. It has to offer more for less—either something that is better, or the same thing at lower cost, or something better at lower cost—to customers who will pay for it. (It is not enough to offer something that is better and cheaper than something else if the latter is not wanted anyway, or if there is an even better alternative to the improved product.)

Both agricultural revolutions—the one around 7,000 BC and that around 1750–1850 AD, provided better food at much lower cost. Any automobile bought today costs a fraction of the price, adjusted for inflation or earnings, that a car cost 50 years ago, yet it is much safer, more comfortable, and stuffed with features, including hundreds or thousands of times more computing power than existed on the whole planet then. We get much more for much less.

Creation is not a mysterious process, confined to the scientific genius, the mad inventor, or the entrepreneur receiving visions from who knows where. Creation can be engineered, if you understand what drives it. Individuals and ideas drive creation. It happens in predictable and repeatable ways. If we understand this, we can create.

Become an 80/20 person

The 80/20 principle enables anyone who is determined, bright, or shrewd to stamp their footprint on the world, to become an 80/20 person. To make something new and popular, to feel that you have achieved something, and to acquire the status and freedom of choice that go with new territory—these are things to relish. This book explores how you can join the revolution.

Notes and references

1 Joseph Moses Juran (1951) *Quality Control Handbook*, McGraw-Hill, New York, pp. 38–9. "The economist Pareto found that wealth was non-uniformly distributed in the same way [as Juran noted about quality losses]. Many other instances can be found—the distribution of crime among criminals, the distribution of accidents among hazardous processes, etc. Pareto's principle of unequal distribution applied to distribution of wealth and to distribution of quality losses."

2 Richard Koch (1997, 1998) *The 80/20 Principle: The Secret of Achieving More with Less*, Nicholas Brealey, London/Currency Doubleday, New York.

3 *Ecclesiastes* 1:9-10 is worth quoting in full:
   "What has been is what will be,
   and what has been done is what will be done;
   and there is nothing new under the sun.

Is there a thing of which it is said,

'See, this is new'?

It has been already,

In the ages before us."

4   As Tachi Kiuchi, the chairman of Mitsubishi America, says, "A microchip's physical content isn't very valuable. Silica is the cheapest and most abundant raw material on the planet—sand. But a microchip—its shape, its design, its unseen artistry—is extremely valuable. Yet it comes from a source that seems almost unlimited—the knowledge and inspiration that we draw from the human spirit and mind. This is the most valuable resource, and the most abundant."

2 The Rise of the Creative Individual

"Give me a single place to stand, and a lever, and I will move the Earth."
Archimedes

The world has never before presented such ripe pickings to the individual creator. Whether you stay within your current firm, start a new one, or become a one-person adventurer, you can create things that other people want. And if you do *that*, you can gain control of your destiny.

I challenge you to create more—much more than you have before, and much more than you think possible. There is an incredibly powerful way in which this can be done, if you know how. To create something new and valuable you must express your individuality and tap into one of the most powerful forces on earth, the 80/20 principle. You must become an 80/20 person.

The rise of 80/20 people

Business and society are being transformed by the fall of the collective and the rise of the individual as the source of both wealth and wellbeing and as the organizing principle of life. This is the rise of 80/20 individuals, 80/20 people. It is the 80/20 revolution—the replacement of capital-ism by a new, twenty-first-century form of team-based individualism.

80/20 people are individuals who express their individuality to create something new and useful to other people. They are not machine-like people who administer the status quo, or people who build machines where the collective institution is more important than the individual.

80/20 individuals and teams are mobile. Their primary loyalty is to themselves and their small team of other individuals, not to an institution. They may build large and valuable organizations, but they know that the organization is there for the creative individual, not the other way round. The institution is their vehicle, not their master. Above all, 80/20 people are idiosyncratic individualists. Although they are single individuals, they have a profound impact.

Who are 80/20 people?

80/20 people cut across all established categories. They are found in all walks of life: in politics, business, social work and not-for-profits, sports, entertainment, the media.

Oprah Winfrey is an 80/20 person. So too are Jeff Bezos, David Bowie, Richard Branson, Warren Buffett, Jim Clark, Bill Clinton, Larry Ellison, Bill Gates, John Grisham, Andy Grove, Tom Hanks, Robert Johnson, Michael Jordan, Nelson Mandela, Ronald Reagan, Steven Spielberg. In her time, Florence Nightingale was an 80/20 person. So were Christoforo Colombo, Henry Ford, Isaac Newton, George Orwell, Mother Teresa, Sam Walton.

By contrast, all those who run the world's organizational machines— armies, states, business organizations—and inherited those machines, did not create or transform them, are not 80/20 people. Those who inher-ited wealth and have not increased it are not 80/20 people. The UK's Queen Elizabeth, for instance, is not an 80/20 person. Neither are Gerald Ford, Al Gore, nor, despite his popularity, George W. Bush. Most of the world's powerful but faceless people are not 80/20 people. Their power is organizational, not personal. They are interchangeable, part of an elite, not individual creators.

80/20 people create, and that is why they matter. Not because of their title or formal role—because of what they do, because they are individuals, not part of a machine.

All successful entrepreneurs are 80/20 people. Entrepreneurs use their individuality to create something new and different and valuable. Many people outside business do precisely the same thing: artists, scientists, writers, broadcasters, stars of sport and screen, creators of popular movements of all kinds. We could think of them as intellectual entrepreneurs, social entrepreneurs, entertainment entrepreneurs, sports entrepreneurs. But the word entrepreneur belongs to business, and stretching it beyond that world does not work well.

Even in business the word entrepreneur is confusing, because creation in business is not confined to entrepreneurs. Many executives in large organizations create huge value as individuals. Creative executives may produce more value as individuals than do many entrepreneurs. One of this book's important subtexts is that creative executives nearly always get seriously short-changed by their organizations. My mission is to encourage such individuals to capture a large chunk of the value they create. If enough creative executives do so, the economy's whole structure could suddenly be transformed.

Creative individuals change the world

John Maynard Keynes, probably the twentieth century's greatest economist, recognized the pivotal role of creative individuals and personal optimism in creating growth and jump-starting economic revolutions. According to Keynes, the enemy of growth is perennial underinvestment. Because people are risk averse and the future is uncertain, there is rarely enough investment. Economic leaps forward occur when for particular reasons—such as the influx of gold from the New World or inventions like the steam engine—individual business people feel unusually confident and expansive.[1]

We can apply Keynes' insight more broadly. Creative individuals literally change the world. Christoforo Colombo discovered the Americas, directly and indirectly creating enormous wealth and handing to Europe leadership of the world for nearly four centuries. The great scientists, from Isaac Newton to Charles Darwin and Albert Einstein, expand and change our mental horizons, shifting our view of the universe and its potentialities. Individual entrepreneurs—think of Andrew Carnegie, Henry Ford, Bill Gates, Konosuke Matsushita, Akio Morita, or Sam Walton—transform whole industries. The process is jerky and lumpy, as we lurch forward by fits and starts courtesy of creative people.

Individuals and their small teams drive progress. Yet behind the flowering and proliferation of individual genius lie two neglected but vital conditions. One is what Keynes called "animal spirits," the feeling that the universe is a wonderful playground that we have barely started to explore. The other is the widespread application of one scientific insight: the 80/20 principle.

Creative individuals and the 80/20 principle

Think of all the billions of people in the world, today and throughout history. Now think of the number of people who have had a significant impact on the world, great thinkers, religious leaders, explorers, soldiers, scientists, politicians, artists. Whatever list we make, there is a very small number of people who have had quite disproportionate impact on our daily lives.

Probably fewer than 1 percent of people have exerted more than 99 percent influence on the world. These creative individuals have changed what went before and what would have happened without them. They have done so not as part of a mass, but as individuals: people taking a divergent view, thinking or doing something that would never have been thought or done collectively.

Would a council of religious leaders have originated Christianity or Islam? Would all the rulers of Europe have decided to sponsor a voyage across the Atlantic to find new lands? Would committees of scientists have decided that the world was round and not flat, or arrived at Newton's laws of motion, Darwin's theory of evolution, or Einstein's laws of relativity?

I don't think we have ever quite understood the process by which individuals create. In this book I present a new theory based around the 80/20 principle. It is obvious that creative people generate value that is many times greater than the average person. The mathematics behind the 80/20 principle suggests that the minority of creative people each produce at least 16 times more than one of the majority of people. This view fits with experience, yet how can it happen? Is a difference of 16 times credible? It's a mind-blowing difference. Even the most brilliant genius is not 16 times smarter than other people.

I think the answer to this paradox lies in our false assumption that intelligence directly creates insight and value. In my view, wealth and wellbeing are created by individuals interacting with a "wealth creation multiple" that multiplies the impact of individual intelligence and effort. The missing link consists in ideas, which are the wealth creation multiple.

The individual wealth creator is not the ultimate source of value; there is something more fundamental going on. We are like fish in the ocean, part of a chain absorbing and creating life, using the most valuable thing in the universe, ideas. All ideas need to be incarnated in products and services. Only individuals and small teams can create, appropriate, develop, and clothe ideas in business reality. The power that individuals have derives very largely from ideas and how well they serve them. This is important because we are only beginning to understand how important ideas are, how to choose between powerful and trivial ideas, how to combine and leverage ideas, and how their potential can best be liberated and renewed.

As we saw in Chapter 1, the 80/20 principle tells us that a few ideas are hugely more powerful than others. Albert Einstein was able to create the theories of relativity not just because he was a genius, but also because he was playing around with powerful ideas, those deriving from early quantum physics. He knew which ideas to select and work on, as well as how to give those ideas a unique twist.

It follows that human creation, while remaining individualistic and inspired, always follows the same pattern. The pattern can be described using the 80/20 principle. The trick is to look beneath or beyond the "average" nature of reality and isolate the few really powerful forces and ideas behind success—to focus on the "vital few" rather than the "trivial many."

Creativity itself cannot be reduced to a cookbook formula. Individual insight and knowledge will always be essential. Yet anyone who has deep knowledge or great instincts about a particular area of endeavor can speed up the process of creation, and be more confident of a very positive result, by using the 80/20 principle. Understanding the principle enables individuals to create more, faster, and with fewer blind alleys. It is my hope that, once the power of the 80/20 principle to help individuals create is understood, many more people will step forward to try their hand at creating something new and valuable. The world can never have too many 80/20 people.

My own experience of creation is in business. Most of my case studies are business creators. You can certainly use this book to help you create a new business venture, but the 80/20 principle applies to all fields of endeavor. The ideas and approaches here are relevant to all 80/20 people and to all creative spheres.

Individuals versus machines

A final and very important link between the 80/20 principle and creative individuals is the recent and probably unstoppable trend favoring individuals over machines, creative people over organizations belonging to other people. Although not everyone would agree, and at first sight it may seem a strange assertion, I believe that we live in a world that increasingly favors individuals rather than collective entities.

Individuals, I argue, are the creators of wealth and wellbeing, and have been for some time. But it does not feel that way. If we were to ask "What drives the economy and its growth?" or "What creates wellbeing?" most people would reply "large companies," "the stock exchange," "capital," "government," or perhaps "voluntary organizations." Very few would simply reply "creative individuals."

If we turn the question around and ask where wealth accumulates, most observers would point to the dazzling market valuations put on our largest corporations. As I write, despite the collapse of some technology and most internet stocks, Microsoft has a value of $286 billion. Our top corporations have never been more valuable and, despite recent falls, most of the world's stock markets are higher than they were five years ago, and many times higher than they were 30 years ago or at any stage before. And in each market, value is concentrated in fewer and fewer stocks. Big business is where value resides. In each industry, there are two or three mega-corporations that control a majority of the market.

In this global economy, where the big get bigger and wealth goes to the big, what place is there for the individual? Capital and corporations rule the roost. Individuals have to fit in with powerful organizations as best they can, both in their working lives and as citizens.

Or do they? Is there another way of interpreting what is happening?

Individuals: the magic, invisible force behind growth

Consider how the economy grows. Does it grow because big companies march ever forward, or because small companies grow from nothing into big companies? The answer is black-and-white. Research by Hewlett-Packard and The Corporate Strategy Board shows that as companies enter the Fortune 50—the 50 largest US corporations—their growth slows down from a range of 9–29 percent a year to 3–4 percent. Looked at over a long period, 91 percent of companies that become big enough to enter the Fortune 50 then slowed down and never grew substantially again through their own endeavors.[2] Acquisitions are evidence of the inability of big business to grow, not the reverse: Gigantic companies have to grow their earnings through acquisitions because they cannot grow themselves.

The economy grows because small companies grow. Behind every small company success story is an individual or small group of individuals. Individuals are at the heart of small company growth. But more: Today individuals are often also at the heart of big company growth.

Take Microsoft, a company that did not exist 30 years ago. Twenty years ago it was worth almost nothing; today, $286 billion. Is Microsoft evidence of corporate hegemony, or of individual enterprise; testimony to the importance of capital and corporations, or individuals?

Microsoft looks like a mega-corporation. It is quoted on the stock exchange and has been, for some time, the most valuable company in the world. But it is not a typical twentieth-century large corporation. At Microsoft there is no separation of ownership from control, the hallmark of managerial capitalism. The chairman, Bill Gates, owns 12.3 percent, other directors another 5 percent, and employees in total more than a third. Microsoft has been made by a few very creative individuals and runs largely for their benefit. It is not on the stock exchange because Microsoft needed capital, but because that route made Mr. Gates and the other founders wealthier than would the alternative.

In the global net worth stakes, Warren Buffett is second only to Bill Gates. Buffett runs America's largest and most successful conglomerate, based in Omaha, of all places. Buffett has a tiny office, employs just a handful of people, and claims to do very little: "Our investment philosophy," he says, "borders on lethargy." How can one individual, supported by a team of trifling size, generate such a fortune? What on earth is going on?

Without our realizing it, the way in which wealth is generated has changed fundamentally over the past 50 years, and at an accelerating rate over the past two decades. Capital and corporations used to be collective instruments, where the system created wealth and the individual executives were interchangeable and therefore dispensable. Now, capital and corporations are individual instruments, available to individuals and used by them for their own purposes. The corporate systems and the capital are now the interchangeable parts; the unique and indispensable element is the individual wealth creator and small teams of creative individuals.

Individualism and the small team

A creative individual needs a small team, even if the team is often just two or three individuals. In 2001, the consulting firm Accenture published a major survey on entrepreneurship, based on nearly 1,000 executives. The study concluded that the popular image of the solitary entrepreneur is a myth: "True entrepreneurship is not a lone pursuit but highly collaborative behavior of critical importance to every nation and organization, whatever its size."

The Accenture findings resonate with the experience of the 80/20 people we will meet throughout this book. These 80/20 people each have their own space, but do not suffer from solitary confinement. Within their little bubbles there is invariably a small team of partners or supporters. One of the marks of 80/20 people is concentration on their distinctive strengths and awareness of their many weaknesses. The weaknesses of 80/20 people require other individuals to counterbalance them; 80/20 people can only be effective by surrounding themselves with others.

Contemporary individualism is not a throwback to the splendid isolation of the rugged and self-reliant nineteenth-century hero, or to Victorian political philosophers such as John Stuart Mill. The new individualism recognizes the social, economic, and intellectual context within which the individual operates, and the enormous importance of the self-selected small team supporting every individual.

This is neither elitist nor zero-sum. Highly idiosyncratic individuals respect, encourage, and nurture individualism in other people. The more different and individualistic we become, the more we call forth and depend on other individuals with utterly different profiles. This is how ecology and society develop, with ever-increasing specialization and interdependence. The days are going when individuals became powerful through building armies of subservient clones. Such tactics may appear to work for a time, but they end up destroying, not creating. True creation requires liberation of the human spirit and the rampant proliferation of every individual's unique potential.

The new society of cooperating individuals

We are used to thinking that wealth and wellbeing come from large organizations, which, however liberal or individualized they claim to become, are inevitably hierarchies.

Our thinking is out of date. Progress today comes from the individual and his or her very small team, linked to other teams of similar composition and complementary skills. Where these other teams sit—whether they are part of the same organization, a different organization, or outside any organization—is becoming irrelevant.

There is an ever-shifting, kaleidoscopic network of individuals and their small teams relating to other individuals and small teams. The units cooperate not because they are told to, nor because they are altruistic, but because they benefit from doing so. Cooperating individuals get rich. The benefits are based on specialization and, ultimately, on individuality.

Can I quickly insert here a note on my terminology in the rest of the book? When I write "individuals," please remember that I mean "individuals and their small teams." It would be tedious if I spelt this out all the time. (I would like to offer a prize for the first person to come up with an elegant word meaning "individual-and-small-team.")

Not fleas versus elephants

Guru Charles Handy has recently written about a world of "fleas and elephants."[3] The "elephants" are large organizations. The "fleas" are what he also calls "independents," one-person bands such as writers, consultants, or artists. He sees the number of independents increasing, as people like him leave organizations to become sole traders. Handy gives them useful advice on how to live outside an organization.

Handy is right that the number of "fleas" is increasing. Yet that is to miss the significance of the rise of the individual. If all individuals did was to leave organizations and become contractors to them, or sell their labor elsewhere, business and society would not change very much.

Individualism would remain confined to the margins of the economy.

80/20 people are not "fleas." 80/20 people are not one-person bands. 80/20 people have a higher ambition than selling their labor themselves. 80/20 people cooperate with each other, and with both "fleas" and "elephants," to create substantial, super-productive new business or social enterprises.

80/20 people add permanently to the stream of progress. They leave behind products or organizations that last, or that lead to even better products and enterprises created by other 80/20 people.

80/20 people are not lonely independents. 80/20 people collaborate with many other individuals to create new organizations. These organizations are not "elephants." They are a new species—call them "jaguars" if you wish, or anything else that is fast and vigorous. But animal metaphors mislead.

Animal analogies are ultimately interchangeable. Each person is unique, as are the organizations they create. The new 80/20 organizations reflect the personality of individuals. The organization serves the individual, not the other way round. 80/20 organizations are the result of collective endeavor, by teams of individuals. The individuals control the collective and the surplus it generates.

Why is the rise of individuals so exciting?

Why am I so excited by this new view of the rise of individuals? Partly because it is a way of viewing reality that makes sense of the fresh evidence that we have so far struggled to fit into our existing categories and ways of thinking.

For example, there has been much talk in the past few years about intellectual capital[4] and its increasingly greater importance than financial capital. The concept is intuitive and useful, yet "real" capital is still the focus of CEOs and financial markets.

How do we explain this paradox? Simply by realizing that intellectual capital belongs to individuals, not to corporations. Intellectual capital can only be created by individuals. Apart from patents, brands, and other legally recognized intellectual property (which have always been important), intellectual capital has little value unless it is renewed by individuals every month or week or day.

The increased importance of intellectual capital helps to explain why individuals are becoming more powerful, and corporate systems less powerful. To try to make intellectual capital a corporate asset, or to count it as one, is fitting new wine into old bottles. Valuable intellectual capital quickly becomes real capital held by individuals. The intellectual capital created by Bill Gates, for example, can be approximated by the value of his personal holding of Microsoft stock.

Never before have so many individuals made a personal difference to the world: not just to the few people immediately around them, but more broadly. Yet I believe that for every individual who creates significant wealth and wellbeing for other people, there are perhaps 10, 20, or 100 individuals who could do so.

One of my main purposes in writing this book is to persuade a large number of individuals to try their hand at creating something big. Very few do this, although most people could, if they really wanted to. I describe how to do it in Part II. It boils down to finding the few things that you are exceptionally good at, finding an idea that fits with your talents and works unusually well, finding other people who can work with you to develop that idea and make it valuable to customers, and using other businesses to do all the hard work for you.

In the old days, the great majority of individuals would have found it difficult or impossible to create a new business. Capital was not available. Management was not available. Technology was not available. Ideas were not available. These essential ingredients had all been monopolized by large corporations, or so it seemed. Most people do not realize that today these barriers are gone. They think creating a business is risky and unpleasant. They are wrong. The barriers are self-imposed, mental maps of a bygone era.

If you want to create something new and valuable, you probably can. All you need are the right ideas, the right people, and reasonable determination and intelligence. (Excess intelligence is more likely to dis-qualify than to help you.)

Another very important point is that many people who have created valuable new businesses have not been rewarded for this. You will meet in this book many examples of executives and other creative individuals who have made a real difference—sometimes measured in tens or even hundreds of millions of dollars—and who have received nothing compa-rable themselves. Sometimes, for social or philanthropic reasons, these productive creators have deliberately and happily given and not received. However, many of my unrewarded creators have been managers working in for-profit corporations, where the benefit of their actions has gone overwhelmingly to passive investors.

Why is this? Because the creators have not been aware of the extent to which they personally have created the value. They imagine that the corporation is the basic source of wealth, and that it is fair that they receive no more than a good salary. I hope to persuade these people—you may be one of them—to use their power to take a fair portion of what they create.

If there is too great a gap between those who create value and those who take it, the economy is distorted and growth is slower than it would otherwise be. If creative individuals are properly rewarded, they will create more, because they have both the incentive and also more capital. And this will encourage other creators to put their best foot forward.

A new phenomenon: the 80/20 billionaire

The 80/20 principle has created a totally new phenomenon: the 80/20 billionaire. The leaders of mega-billion corporations like Black Entertainment Television[5] or Oracle or Goldman Sachs are billionaire owners as well as executives.

These corporations look to the untutored eye just like General Motors or IBM, differing, apparently, only in their higher value. But the new owner-managed corporations, where the executives enjoy not just options or tiny stakes but billions of dollars of stock, are a species apart.

They are instruments for their founders, impudently tapping the capital markets not for capital but for a price for their stock. Without the 80/20 principle, this new breed of individual-centered corporations could not have existed.

Although it may seem preposterous, what Bill Gates and many other billionaires have done, you can do too, although probably on a more modest scale. You don't need to be a technology genius, or even a high school dropout. You do need to use the 80/20 principle creatively.

Favoring individuals, not big business

During the twentieth century, the 80/20 principle was mainly used by large corporations to reinforce their monopoly or semi-monopoly status in selected markets. Fewer than 20 percent of the firms in any market ended up with more than 80 percent market share. Typically, each global market ended up with two or three dominant US producers, and one or two from other countries. The mainstream automobile market, for instance, reduced to Ford, General Motors, and Chrysler, with Toyota as the main non-US competitor. It was universally imagined that the 80/20 principle would favor corporate size and concentration.

I was not immune from this assumption. When I published *The 80/20 Principle* in 1997, the book applied the 80/20 principle to work, and to individuals, but not to individuals at work. The work section assumed that corporate executives would apply the principle for the benefit of their firms. I broke new ground by applying the 80/20 principle to individuals, but this was to encourage personal effectiveness and happiness, not to start or develop an individual-centered enterprise.

With *The 80/20 Revolution*, we move to a different world. Here, individuals can turn an existing market upside down by focusing on just one small part of it—the most profitable part. Instead of one firm monopolizing the market, we look for the most profitable 20 percent of the market, that which yields 80 percent of the profit. We find the most profitable 20 percent (or 5 percent, or 1 percent) of customers, suppliers, employees, geographic regions, products, and activities. For instance, if all the profit can be made by branding, why bother to manufacture, distribute, or sell?

What happens in this new world? Markets fly apart. What was one market can become literally hundreds. Nevertheless, a majority of profit is made in just a few, maybe only one or two, of these niches.

Intel and Microsoft between them can make the majority of profit in a market, yet leave all the donkey work between chip manufacture and software production—the vast majority of physical activity and invest-ment in the PC market—to other firms.

Because new players don't need to be in every product or every activ-ity, they can select the best playgrounds. A small minority of activity makes a large majority of profits. Thus the 80/20 principle is turned against the old, broad-line monopolists, against old corporations, and in favor of individuals who start new businesses.

What value is all that sunk investment, when a smart individual can use the 80/20 principle, and very small amounts of capital, to capture the sweet spots in a market? The investment becomes a trap. The large firm and its hierarchy become obligations, not assets. The 80/20 principle opens up whole new worlds, especially and particularly for small firms, new firms, and above all for individuals.

The essence of the 80/20 principle is that it takes a large arena—an average—and finds the best seats in that arena. It looks for the smallest possible slivers of greatest possible value. In business, the smallest sliver of value creation becomes the imaginative individual—and the greatest value can also be captured by the individual, usually through a corporation that he or she owns.[6]

Are we near a tipping point?

A "tipping point" occurs when a new product, trend, or behavior "tips over" from being confined to a small subculture or area to becoming a mass phenomenon. The tipping point is an invisible line that, once crossed, changes everything, maybe for ever.[7]

A disease, like the plague or AIDS, becomes an epidemic. Democracy becomes a force than cannot be denied. Pre-marital sex or ecstasy becomes part of youth culture. Water becomes steam. The mobile phone becomes ubiquitous.

Is the rise of the individual near a tipping point? In Part III I claim that it is. I look at previous economic transformations, from nomadic hunter-gatherer society to settled agricultural society based on feudalism; from that to the early industrial world, based on small owner-producers and free markets; and the transition during the twentieth century to large hierarchical, managed corporations financed by stock exchanges and run by salaried managers.

I argue that the accelerating trends of the last 20 years—especially the detachment of value from assets and ownership, the growth of outsourcing and alliances, the re-emergence of owner-managers, and the creation of new economic systems that transcend the boundaries of individual enterprises—all give power and wealth to creative individuals, and indicate the potential for a quite different economic system. If we don't cross the tipping point, individuals will get rich or take nonmonetary rewards within our familiar economic system.

But if we do cross the tipping point, what would that mean? I talk about the replacement of capitalism by a new type of team-based individualism. What would that look like?

We cannot know for sure. The nature of dramatic transitions is that they create something qualitatively different, which cannot be anticipated by simple extrapolation of past trends. How was anyone to know in advance that cultivating plants and rearing animals in captivity would lead to kings and priests and serfdom, as well as to great architecture and empires? That feudal society would be rendered obsolete and absurd by the steam engine? Or that the management necessary for railroads would lead to mass production, total war, rampant bureaucracy, and the consumer society?

Nevertheless, I have my hunches that we could see some shocking changes. Centering the economy and society around individuals must, on balance, be a good thing. But what if it were to trigger en route a wholesale and permanent collapse of world stock markets? No major economic and social change, even one broadly benign, is devoid of destructive dislocations.

Navigating the rest of the book

Part II, The Nine Essentials of 80/20 Success, shows how you can create something new and valuable. Each chapter is devoted to one of the nine essentials. Part II is studded with cameos of real 80/20 people who are creative individualists, but always teamed up with other people to complement their unique strengths.

Part III, The 80/20 Revolution, shifts gear, from the practical details of how individuals can create to the consequences of such actions at the level of the corporation and the economy. I show how the individual-centered world is emerging; how, in fact, the world has already changed fundamentally without anyone noticing.

Notes and references

1 My account of Keynes' thinking owes much to Professor Skidelsy's landmark biography. See Robert Skidelsky (1992) *John Maynard Keynes: Volume Two, The Economist as Saviour, 1920–1937*, Macmillan, London, especially p. 335.

2 See Don Laurie (2001) *Venture Catalyst: The Five Strategies for Accelerating Corporate Growth*, Nicholas Brealey, London/Perseus Publishing, Cambridge, MA.

3 Charles Handy (2001) *The Elephant and the Flea: Looking Backwards to the Future*, Hutchinson, London.

4 For the best introduction to the subject, see Thomas A. Stewart (1997) *Intellectual Capital: The New Wealth of Organizations*, Nicholas Brealey, London. The erroneous subtitle says it all: *The truth is that the new and most valuable parts of intellectual capital belong to individuals, not to corporations.*

5 Robert Johnson, the richest African-American chief executive, founded BET (Black Entertainment Television) in 1985. He recently sold it to Viacom for $2.3 billion in Viacom stock (Viacom also paid $570 million in assuming

BET debt). Johnson is an excellent example of an 80/20 leader, driven by his vision.

6 This thought derives from the work of The Boston Consulting Group, which used to be the great advocate of industrial concentration, but which has moved with (or ahead of) the times in advocating the "deconstruction" (blowing up) of monolithic markets by new competitors. See the excellent book by Philip Evans and Thomas S. Wurster (2000) *Blown to Bits: How the New Economics of Information Transforms Strategy*, Harvard Business School Press, Boston.

7 See Malcolm Gladwell (2000) *The Tipping Point: How Little Things Can Make a Big Difference*, Little, Brown, New York.

Part II

The Nine Essentials of 80/20 Success

How to enjoy and benefit from Part II

Each chapter contains one of the nine essentials of 80/20 success.

Chapters 3 to 6 focus on identifying the new enterprise that is right for you and that will make huge returns for you and high returns for your backers and supporters. We will explore:

- ❖ Your most creative arena (Chapter 3).
- ❖ The best new idea for the enterprise (Chapter 4).
- ❖ The vital elements that will make it super-profitable (Chapter 5).
- ❖ How the dimension of time can jump-start rewarding innovation (Chapter 6).

As you read, imagine a variety of possible new ventures that you might create. By the end of Chapter 6, you will have visualized several potential new enterprises, and decided which one to build.

Don't jump to conclusions. You may already have a prospective venture in mind. Slow down. Examine myriad possibilities. Toy with many permutations of different ideas.

Chapters 7 to 10 focus on the key ingredients for getting your venture started:

- ❖ People (Chapter 7).
- ❖ Your current firm (Chapter 8).
- ❖ Other firms (Chapter 9).
- ❖ Capital (Chapter 10).

Chapter 11 tells you how to reach the second stage of growth and make a killing.

Confine yourself to one chapter at a time. Mull over the ideas and revisit them before moving on.

Use a good friend and/or a prospective business partner to help you. Read each chapter on your own, get the friend or partner to do the same, and then have a session to share and refine your findings for each chapter.

Relish the challenge! Start creating now!

3 *Enlist Your Most Creative 20 Percent*

"This above all: to thine own self be true,
And it follows as the night the day,
Thou can'st not then be false to any man."

William Shakespeare, Hamlet

To thine own self be true—but which self should you be true to?

The self that spends a huge amount of time and sweat getting nowhere? The self that engages in destructive patterns of behavior? The self that follows the crowd (all of us, saints and lunatics only excepted, spend much or most of our time conforming to the dictates of others)? Our automatic self? The self that achieves nothing out of the ordinary? The self that could just as well not be a self at all?

No. The self to which we must be true is our really distinctive and productive self, our unique self, our imaginative, positive and creative self, the 20 percent or less of ourselves that contributes more than 80 percent of our impact and happiness.

First we have to find this self, to be aware of the powerful vital few characteristics within ourselves. Then we have to nurture and grow this 20 percent. Only then can we use it to make the world and ourselves richer.

The 20 percent spike

What makes a great chief executive or other "building" leader is what psychologists call the "spike," and I call the "20 percent spike." The spike is a distinctive strength that is unusually powerful. The idea is to train and develop the spike to Olympian standards.

Do corporate psychologists, who determine whether you or another short-listed candidate will get the top job, look for well-rounded team players or for oddballs? Intriguingly, the latter. The psychologist wants unusual characters, with a few fantastic strengths. If you have these, he or she couldn't care less about a long laundry list of things you can't do well, or even do at all.

Gurnek Bains, head of YSC, a leading firm of business psychologists, explains: "Any significant leader is not well-rounded. They're all quite different, slightly idiosyncratic characters. The best directors have huge spikes and equally large downsides."[1]

Psychoanalyst Michael Maccoby agrees. He highlights today's "superstar" leaders and draws attention to their lopsided traits: "Today's CEOs—superstars such as Bill Gates, Andy Grove, Steve Jobs, Jeff Bezos, and Jack Welch—hire their own publicists, write books, grant spontaneous interviews, and actively promote their personal philosophies ... [they] closely resemble the personality type that Sigmund Freud dubbed narcissistic."[2]

Maccoby says that such "productive narcissists" have tremendous vision and self-belief, yet are anything but team players. Most would not score well on emotional intelligence or the ability to listen to other people.

The downside is taken care of by finding other people who can deal with those areas. Not all 80/20 people are "productive narcissists," but many of the new superstars are effective precisely because they are unbalanced. Their 20 percent spike is strong enough to see them through; although it is notable that successful leaders of this ilk have a team of other people clearing up the mess around them.

Outsource your 80 percent

One of the most important recent trends in business is outsourcing. Companies that outsource get other companies to take on activities in which they are not world class, and/or functions that give a much lower return on capital. Ideally, firms outsource the "trivial many" 80 percent of tasks and put all their energy into their "vital few" 20 percent of undertakings.

People can do precisely the same thing. The concept is the same as for corporate outsourcing. Find the 20 percent (or less) that you are out-standingly good at, then ask other people to perform the rest.

At least on one level, that of time, the rich and famous have always done this. You don't catch Madonna standing in line at the supermarket or passport office. Heads of state tend to spend less time fuming in traf-fic jams than the rest of us. Celebrities pack several lives into one: They live more intensely, devoid of the dross that bogs us down (they may create their own dross, but that is another story.)

We can all export large chunks of ourselves. If you're not good at something, don't do it. Find someone else to do it, or forget about it alto-gether. Why work hard to become mediocre at something? There are bet-ter uses of your time, your energy, your essential self.

Individuals have very different 20 percent spikes

This is a trite but neglected, vital truth. Of all the billions of people on earth, only identical twins have the same genetic material. And even iden-tical twins have different experiences, inclinations, partners, and emo-tions. Humankind is the most differentiated and specialized of all the world's species. There are "individual" ants and antelopes, but individual-ity reaches its zenith with humans.

Yet we spend most of our lives denying our individuality, trying to pretend that we are just like everyone else. Isn't that weird?

Creative individuals are different. They have more individuality. More precisely: They use their individuality more. They are aware of it. They give it more headroom. They cultivate it. They know where it can be used most effectively.

Creative individuals have less need to fit in. They make fewer concessions to "reality," the reality defined by other people up to that time.

George Bernard Shaw knew this: "The reasonable man adapts himself to the world. The unreasonable one persists in trying to adapt the world to himself. Therefore all progress depends on the unreasonable man." For unreasonable, read creative.

If you want to create, you first have to find and nurture your 20 percent spike. If you want to create a new business, don't start by thinking about the business. Start by thinking about yourself.

The story of Rachel

Rachel is a slim, good looking 51-year-old, who looks at least 10 years younger. She rides a bicycle and lives with a large and indeterminate number of cats. She has a weakness for fast cars.

For eight years, she has been the chief executive of a branded womenswear business. Under her tenure, sales have doubled, yet profits have multiplied 15 times. Her return on capital is 50–60 percent and she hasn't required any new capital; all her expansion capital has been internally generated. She has provided her parent company with copious dividends.

Rachel inherited one venerable but near-dead brand, which she has revived and rejuvenated. She has launched two successful brands from scratch.

For a real-world, low-tech, rag-trade affair, Rachel's concern is surprisingly virtual. Unlike other garment suppliers in the same group, her division outsources all manufacturing. "Why would I want to manufacture," she asks, "when that's such a low-return activity?" Her division's core competencies are design and selling, but it has little capital tied up in either. The clothes are retailed through department store concessions. Rachel pays a rent based on turnover, profits, and space occupied, but effectively uses the department stores' capital. She has hired a high-powered design director, yet most of the design work is outsourced.

Rachel fascinates me for reasons I'll explain later and we're going to track her throughout Part II. How did she get started?

"I left school as soon as I could," Rachel explains. "I was no good at anything except math. I suppose I was bored. I couldn't see how my subjects were relevant to what I was going to do.

"One thing I always loved was clothes. I couldn't afford to buy many good clothes, so I decided to sell them instead. My first job was working in a very large department store in Miami. I loved the atmosphere, it was like a huge family. The merchandise was very varied and there was always something going on. These were all things I had never been exposed to. I started to understand that 'things' could be beautiful. That style and taste were qualities you could develop.

"As part of my training, I moved from department to department. First cosmetics and perfumery. Then jewelry. Then trendy fashion, lots from Europe, like Mary Quant. Eventually I made it to the Designer room. This was fantastic, beautifully made clothes in fantastic fabrics at astronomic prices. Selling to rich women was great fun!

"I wasn't supposed to do it, it wasn't my job, but one day I found myself calculating the profit margin on what we sold. I looked at the invoices and noticed that certain types of merchandise carried fatter margins. It was nearly always the most expensive garments.

"In a way this was natural, people who could afford more wanted the best and didn't care what it cost. But I remember thinking, 'This is really peculiar. These clothes are the best ones to sell, the most expensive, and yet they take little more effort to sell, sometimes less effort, than the cheaper merchandise.' So, if our department wants to take more cash, we should put all our sales push into the dearer stuff. But, you know, it's also true that the percentage margin on the clothes is greatest. So we win both ways. We take more money, but we also make more profit for each dollar we sell. That's when I decided that I should always try hardest to sell the top of our range.

"I noticed another thing. The worst times were when we had to mark down the dresses and suits. And we always had to mark down more than we expected, I mean, both more garments and higher markdowns to shift them. We were always too optimistic, or rather our directors were. Sometimes I wondered how we could make money at all.

"I decided that if ever I got to be the boss, I would be pessimistic. I would expect to sell less at full price, and more at big markdowns. That way I would make more profit than expected, not less.

"You might say that I was day-dreaming. A girl with no credentials would never become the boss. But it's a funny thing. I knew I could do it, I knew that if I became the boss I would be a great boss. It wasn't boasting, I never said anything to anyone else, not even to my best friend. But I knew that I could do it, I knew that I had flair in selecting clothes, and I knew I could do the sums better than anyone else seemed to be able to. I knew it was me. I would be more 'me' if I was the managing director than if I was the sales clerk.

"So eventually I decided. 'Rachel,' I said to myself, 'you will become the boss.' I had fantasies about being Cinderella: 'You will go to the ball.' And I did. The most difficult part about my current job was getting there. It's been downhill from then. Oh dear, am I tempting fate?"

Creative people are not alienated

Rachel tells me, "It's really odd, but I really feel myself when I'm at [she mentions the place she works]. In fact, I'm more myself there than I am at home. I can express myself more. The work, the people, and me ... they fit together. You say it's difficult to create. I don't agree. When I'm there, I find it the easiest thing in the world."

To create, you must belong. If you work for a firm where you can't be yourself, you may create, but only against the grain. You could create much more someplace else.

Imagine the setting where you could be most fertile. Then create it!

The story of Bjorn-Ingvar

One of my best friends has a Swedish friend, let us call him Bjorn-Ingvar. In the early 1980s he was happily employed as a junior professor of English at Göteborg University. He was also a loyal member of his local Lutheran mission church. The church had a tiny little business publishing prayer books, making no money. Because Bjorn-Ingvar was a professor, the church asked him to look after this enterprise on a part-time, unpaid basis. Bjorn-Ingvar agreed, combining it with his university job.

Bjorn-Ingvar soon realized that the economics of publishing depended on having a few titles that sold exceptionally well. His prayer books would never fit this bill. So he looked for one or two secular titles that he could take on, although always ones with a wholesome, Christian bias. It turned out that Bjorn-Ingvar had an eye for unlikely bestsellers.

Soon the activities of the little publishing house demanded more time. So Bjorn-Ingvar, because this was a good cause and something he enjoyed, gave up his professor's salary and accepted a small honorarium from the church to run the publishing house.

Soon the firm's reputation grew among Swedish booksellers: Bjorn-Ingvar's books always sold well. Given his channel into the booksellers, he now looked for successful English brands that he could distribute. Again, because he chose the brands very selectively, this business grew and was very profitable.

By the start of the 1990s, when my friend met him, Bjorn-Ingvar had started to buy up other Swedish publishing houses, but always specialist firms such as those publishing computer manuals. The publishing house was now very much larger than the church that had founded it. Without any capital, without any corporate structure, and initially without any managers, Bjorn-Ingvar had created a business worth tens of millions of dollars.

And still Bjorn-Ingvar was on pretty much the same honorarium, adjusted for inflation, that he had accepted 10 years earlier for supervising the production of a few prayer books. His pay was linked to that of church ministers, well below the average Swedish wage. "I work for the cause and for the church," he told my friend. "If I have created a business worth millions, is this more valuable than the work of a pastor who tends to people's souls?"

Today the business Bjorn-Ingvar created—Libris Media AB—is a major Swedish publishing house, run by professional managers with large salaries. Bjorn-Ingvar left a few years ago to create another small publishing enterprise, this time on his own account. Yet it is clear he is not mainly motivated by money. He told my friend, "I just love building businesses, I love this one just the same as the church business in its early days. What I really enjoy is doing what I do well, which is finding books and related brands of high standards that will have great popular appeal."

The story of Olivo

Olivo Boscariot is a Frenchman of Italian background who lived in Paris as a self-employed picture restorer. When his first child was born, he and his wife wanted more space so they moved to the small medieval town of Provins. Though they loved living there, there was one drawback: no pictures to restore.

Olivo eked out a living as a night watchman. But he became fascinated by the medieval floor tiles on display in the town museum. He knew nothing about ceramics, yet after three attempts managed to get a grant from the local government, together with some support from industrial combine Saint Gobain, to set up artisanal production of medieval floor tile replicas. The government grant specified that he should only employ those, like himself, on the lowest scale of unemployment benefit.

That was in 1992. Now, Olivo's business exports tiles to the US and the UK, as well as having major contracts for public buildings all over France.

Although his business makes money, this is not Olivo's main interest. "I love the tiles themselves," he says, "and I knew that this business would reflect what I do best. My main satisfaction today is helping the lowest of the unemployed set themselves and their families on their feet again. I look for those whom everyone else thinks are unemployable, but whom I know can become interested in the tiles. If they like the tiles, I know the people can be salvaged."

Olivo has an almost religious fervor about helping the desperate unemployed. "Over the past nine years," he tells me, "my business has saved 50 such people." "Saved" is a strong word to use, but it is appropriate. "Typically they stay with me for two or three years, and learn so much that they then go off themselves into the productive economy. Many of them start their own little businesses. My prayer is that they will then do what I am doing, recycling other 'hopeless' people into work that they enjoy and whose products give pleasure to many people."

Perhaps because of his medieval setting, Olivo reminds me of finders of the great monastic orders. They also concentrated on their 20 percent spike, pursuing their passion and saving other people. Today we would classify them as not-for-profit entrepreneurs. The category doesn't matter. What does matter is that like Olivo, Benedict, Francis, and Dominic all created something new and valuable, something that reflected their own vision and the essence of their individuality.

The story of Jamie

One of the last places you would expect a young and junior individual to be able to make a huge economic difference is the British Broadcasting Corporation (BBC). The "Beeb" is a monolithic bureaucracy still financed through the license fee, set by government, which has to be paid by anyone who watches a television in the UK. But the power of 80/20 people can reach even into the Beeb's deep recesses.

When 30-year-old Jamie Reeve, a friend and former business partner, joined the BBC in the mid-1990s, I thought he was crazy; he would become frustrated and make no impact. But I reckoned without his 20 percent spike. Jamie was passionately interested in two subjects: broadcasting and the internet. In the early 1990s he had told me how important the internet would become to business (I ignored him). When he joined the BBC, his objective—which was nothing to do with his job there—was to get the BBC to use its content online.

"I was probably about number 105 in the BBC management hierarchy," he tells me, "but I knew that John Birt, the Director-General, was a creative individual too and I had an idea. What if I could organize a trip for him to go to Silicon Valley and Seattle and meet all the movers and shakers, and get him excited about the prospects?" Jamie not only succeeded in selling the trip idea, but, to his surprise, John Birt insisted that he come along too.

"I will never forget that trip in July 1997," Jamie continues, "Imagine. Just John Birt, Bill Gates, and me, sitting as close together as we are now, talking for two hours about what the internet was doing, and how valuable the Beeb's content was. By the time we came back John was completely sold on the idea."

In November 1997 BBC Online was launched. It is now the most successful content site outside the US, with about 10 million users worldwide and 300 million page impressions a month. Industry observers guesstimate a value of perhaps $1–2 billion if BBC Online were sold today.

Jamie and John Birt have left the BBC. John Birt now chairs the Lynx specialist media venture capital fund, backed by Virgin and Bear Stearns, where Jamie is a partner.

How to enlist your most creative 20 percent

1 Identify your 20 percent spike
Psychologists stress that self-awareness is difficult, and there are various techniques for becoming more self-aware.[3] Yet identifying your 20 percent spike is in fact a great deal easier than becoming aware of your full 100 percent. You may not be aware of all your defects and downsides, but the chances are that you know what turns you on!

By all means use a firm of vocational or business psychologists to help you, but below are some prompts to introspection and feedback from associates that will give you at least 80 percent of the answer.

Ask yourself the following questions and record your answers. Then repeat the exercise with about a dozen people who know you well and whom you trust to give accurate feedback: your life partner, close friends, business partners, your boss (if you have one and trust him or her), some peers, and a few people who work for you.

THE 20 PERCENT SPIKE QUESTIONNAIRE

QUESTION	YOUR PERSONAL ANSWER
❖ What sort of thing really excites [name]? What have you heard [him/her] be most passionate about? [Do not confine this to work-related matters.]	
❖ Imagine that [name] becomes famous in [his/her] lifetime. What possible things might [he/she] become celebrated for?	
❖ What is the single most distinctive thing about [name], that defines above all [his/her] individuality? What is most different and idiosyncratic about [him/her]?	
❖ What do you think [name] would be happiest and most fulfilled doing?	
❖ What one thing is [name] best at, and better at than anyone else you know?	

QUESTION	YOUR PERSONAL ANSWER
❖ What occupation or role do you think [name] is best suited to?	
❖ Think laterally about a different new arena or activity that [name] might be excellent at, preferably far removed from [his/her] current one. Be creative and surprising, perhaps not even entirely serious.	
❖ If [name] were to start a new venture that becomes amazingly successful, what might that new enterprise be? Use your imagination.	

2 Nurture your 20 percent spike

Once you've decided what your 20 percent spike is, you have to train, develop, and hone it until it has reached Olympian standard. As with any skill, daily practice is most important. Do more of what you do best. Do it every day, every way. Study, read, talk, experiment—all based around your 20 percent spike. Meet other people who are excellent exponents of the same or similar attributes. Compare notes. Feed your passion. Accentuate your own distinctive approach, so that you have an inimitable and unique style.

Your 20 percent spike and your new venture

We will see in the next few chapters that the nature of business opportunity is greatly misunderstood. The raw materials of business success—powerful ideas and great people—are abundant. But the idea of the 20 percent spike implies that you should not be looking for any old opportunity, however great it may be.

The point is to look for the specific opening that you will exploit better and more creatively than anyone else. It is not enough to find a terrific and profitable endeavor. It is not sufficient to find something that you can do very well. Your destiny is to find a venture that is more suited to you than to anybody else, something that nobody could do as well as you. Otherwise, somebody may, and all your labors will be overtaken.

What about the 80–99 percent of things you're not brilliant at?

You need other people: Partners probably, supporters certainly. Your Olympian strength—the 20 percent, or more likely the 1 percent—requires the 80–99 percent to be supplied by other people. You need a small team to be effective.

It has taken me some time to realize this. I used to think that the 20 percent was all we should worry about, but now I see that one can't just have the 20 percent. As a perceptive reviewer of *The 80/20 Principle* commented, the meat in a hamburger (the 20 percent) needs the bread roll (the 80 percent), or it's not a hamburger. This does not invalidate the 80/20 principle. We should still focus on the vital 20 percent (or less), but we should ensure that the 80 percent is also well catered for, by other people who are part of the same team. My 80 percent may be your 20 percent.

In any case, it is often difficult to say precisely what one's 20 percent is; and both the 20 percent and the 80 percent change over time as we evolve and the context changes. The cardinal point is to be aware of the new 20 percent emerging within ourselves, and give it priority and support—from ourselves and from our small team. There is a crucial emotional side to this too. Human beings need social support. Like genes, our 20 percent needs to be protected and incarnated and encouraged to evolve within robust and hospitable social contexts.

Nurture your team: When they are not equity partners, they should be thought of as supporters, not as employees. Your success must be their success as well—they must benefit from being part of your world, just as you benefit from them being part of yours.

Do you need partners?

You have to decide whether your strength is broad enough to sustain success in your intended area.

The test is this: If your 20 percent spike is a sufficient basis for a successful new undertaking, you don't need partners. If it isn't, you do.

For instance, my first venture was a management consultancy specializing in business strategy. My 20 percent spike, I believed, was strategic insight; I could answer questions such as "What should this firm really be doing?" Yet I didn't think this was a sufficiently broad basis for a successful firm competing with the likes of McKinsey, Bain, or Boston Consulting. Specifically, there were two essential ingredients that I lacked: the ability to do "heavy-duty" quantitative analysis, and train other consultants in this; and the ability to lead and manage a serious professional firm. Without these ingredients, I could have kept myself and a few employees busy, but not built a significant and enduring firm. Happily, I had two partners who covered the bases I couldn't: Iain Evans was a world-class analyst, and Jim Lawrence a leader of Olympian stature.

If you need partners, what must their 20 percent spikes be? To pose the question is to answer it. Their 20 percent spikes must comprise whatever is necessary for the unique success of the new venture that you cannot provide yourself.

Deciding what to create

When you have decided on the inimitable power that you and your partner(s) have as individuals, you're ready to move on and decide what you will create. Chapters 4 to 6 show how the 80/20 principle can guide your choice of business domain.

Notes and references

1 Quoted in Robert Winnett (2001) "Inside the minds of Britain's top bosses," *Sunday Times*, London, 1 July.

2 Michael Maccoby (2000) "Narcissistic leaders: The incredible pros, the inevitable cons," *Harvard Business Review*, January–February.

3 Broadly, self-awareness can be increased by three methods. One is to be genuinely open to feedback from the people around you. The second is to organize the feedback process, covering a wide variety of topics in a questionnaire and getting the feedback from as many relevant people as possible. The third is to go through an outside process using a psychological model. One unique method is an anonymous web-based system called Lifepi that enables you to receive feedback from a qualified psychologist without any personal intrusion at all; for more information, visit www.lifepi.com. Readers should note that I have an indirect financial interest in Lifepi. For more on self-awareness see Chapter 4 of Jonathan Yudelowitz, Richard Koch, and Robin Field (2002) *Smart Things to Know About Leadership*, Capstone, Oxford.

4 *Enlist and Mutate Great Ideas*

"There is no force on earth so powerful as an idea whose time has come."
Victor Hugo

Every business can be described in words. In some ways, the idea behind the business is its most fundamental definition. James Champy has expressed this view trenchantly:

> *"People like to think that businesses are built of numbers (as in the 'bottom line'), or forces (as in 'market forces'), or things ('the product'), or even flesh and blood ('our people'). But this is wrong. Businesses are made of ideas— ideas expressed as words."*

Champy is exaggerating. Enterprises have all these attributes at once: They are numbers, forces, things, people, and ideas. Businesses are living, moving entities that we can create and capture using all these things.

Nevertheless, there is great power in viewing enterprises as ideas. An idea can be expressed in numbers; in a mathematical formula; in a graph; in a picture; or, with greatest versatility, in words. If numbers are the music, words are the lyrics of business.

For those who like mathematical expressions, we can write:

Any enterprise = Ideas   + Numbers
Any enterprise = Lyrics   + Music

This chapter is going to concentrate on the ideas behind the business: the words, the lyrics. (We will deal with the numbers in Chapter 5.) In applying the 80/20 principle, we will look in this chapter for the unique new idea for your venture. This is not as difficult as it sounds. The truth is that in any sphere of business there are just a few powerful ideas. Latch on to one, two, or three of these, produce a variant that is uniquely adapted to your abilities and market, and you have the germ of a successful new enterprise.

We will use deductive reasoning: We start with a general law of success, based around ideas and the 80/20 principle, and derive variants. Our quest is the vital few ideas that can drive 80/20 people to unique success.

Business as ideas

Every new business must start with an idea. What is your new business idea? And how can the 80/20 principle help you arrive at it?

The progressive, useful, dynamic part of life consists of the amazingly productive, small minority of forces that produces nearly all the results. But the 80/20 principle is also itself dynamic, leading to new results from new minorities of forces. Within any productive 20 percent, there is also another 20 percent, and within that another 20 percent. This becomes most apparent over time. Really fantastic improvements come in a time series, where the process is repeated over and over. The semiconductor and the microchip are brilliant examples: Astounding results come from a successful process, such as miniaturization, that is replicated ceaselessly.

The trivial 80 percent may appear to be waste, but if we view the process as dynamic each 80 percent is necessary. Without the trivial many, the vital few cannot emerge.

Life is an experiment. Unless we go down blind alleys, we will never find the few alleys that are not blind. We are stuck in a maze—the 80/20 principle signposts the exit.

Natural selection and business genes

Nature is wildly inefficient, but that doesn't matter. How could today's complex array of different life forms, the lush economy of plants and animals, possibly have emerged? By going through zillions of mazes and blind alleys, and untold dimensions of waste; through the progressive, slow but relentless emergence of "vital fews" out of "trivial manys."

Biologist Richard Dawkins estimates that history has witnessed "some three billion branches to the river of DNA,"[1] three billion different species. For every species alive today, 99 have lived but become extinct. This is a 99/1 relationship—each successful story consumes 99 drafts.

Charles Darwin's fantastic account of natural selection in 1859[2] cannot be bettered as a description of how the 80/20 principle operates over time.[3] The trivial many—unsuccessful prototypes—die and give way to the vital few successful prototypes. These themselves give birth to many variants, and the environment selects a vital few of these to survive and give birth to many variants, in a never-ending chain. At each stage there is a minority of powerful forces. These give rise to another universe (100 percent) of forces, of which a vital few (20 percent or fewer) survive, which give birth to another batch (100 percent) of descendants, which in turn...

The dynamic 80/20 process of natural selection is an incredibly apt way of viewing ideas. Genes are what drives the reproductive process of natural selection. Genes are actually pure information—they are ideas—and all ideas work like genes.

Like plants and animals, humans would be useless machines without the genes that drive us.[4] Similarly, ideas—what I call "business genes"— drive success in business.[5]

Business genes are packets of beneficial economic information, ideas that are useful for business. Success in life comes from having good genes.[6] Individual creatures end up with good genes if they are the best available vehicles for those genes. Likewise, success in business comes from great business ideas, and from being the best available vehicle for those ideas in a specific market.

Business genes are useful ideas about which products and services to provide, to which customers, in what ways; about which suppliers to use and how to produce what is offered to customers; about how to deliver the product offerings; about how to find the right partners and employees and coordinate them; about how to make an economic surplus and a higher return on capital than had previously been possible; and about anything else that defines a business and gives it potential to create new wealth.

Which business ideas are the vital few?

The trick is to identify the "vital few" ideas that can bring success to you. This has two sides. One, you need great ideas that have proved themselves. Two, you need ideas that fit your 20 percent spike.

Great ideas always exist in a chain of successful ideas. Successful ideas have many ancestors and many descendants. The best place to look for your new business idea is in the minority of ideas that have already proven themselves to be highly successful—in the 20 percent or fewer, in the vital few business genes. Then experiment. Tweak the idea in a large number of different ways until you find the vital few or the vital one variant that makes you most successful.

But great ideas will only stay with you if you are the best possible vehicle for them. If you can't take the ideas and make better use of them than anybody else, fortune will desert you. Choose ideas that resonate with your most creative 20 percent, ideas that find their destiny in you.

Competition at the level of ideas

The most important competition in business—the winnowing of the trivial many and the triumph of the vital few—takes place at the level of business ideas. This is true for products, for technologies, for management techniques, and for every other form of serious competition, where there are few winners and many losers, and where the winners are replaced by even better versions of themselves.

Real competition in any product, for instance, is not between competing firms or even their products, but between *ideas* for the products. For every product that reaches the market alive and well, many will have been discarded before reaching the drawing board, many will have died on the drawing board, many will have been scrapped during the development phase, many will not have made it through the test market, and many will not have had economic repurchase rates.

Successful products end up in a museum

Good ideas are especially vulnerable to the operation of the 80/20 principle. For every good idea, better versions of the same idea, or variants serving a similar purpose, arise and kill the original. Probably the most useful single new idea of the early twentieth century was the Model T Ford: By giving the middle classes and ordinary working people the freedom to move, it transformed society. The point about the Model T, as David Hounshell, the historian of mass production, stresses, is that it "was as much an idea as it was an automobile ... an unchanging car for the masses."[7]

Where do we find Model Ts today? Not on the road, but in a car museum. Why? Not because the Model T failed—it is dead because it succeeded. This wonderful idea has been killed by thousands of new, better ideas, all linearly descended from the first one, and all intent on killing their parents and siblings.

What matters is not the product, or the firm that produces it, but the idea behind it. The idea of mass-market automobile transportation found many other vehicles to take it forward.

Combine and tweak previous ideas

Every great business innovation has built on earlier great ideas, and added a novel twist. For the Model T automobile, it started with the market concept: "An unchanging car for the masses" to be sold at a low price.

How did Henry Ford create a low price? He took ideas that had already worked in other products for other people. He took the idea of production scale from Andrew Carnegie, who had proved 30 years earlier that if you built steel mills many times the size of earlier ones, you could reduce the cost to a fraction of the previous level. In building his gigantic car plant, which opened on New Year's Day, 1910, at Highland Park, Detroit, Ford took three ideas that had proved successful elsewhere: moving lines of work in progress; special-purpose machinery that turned out modular parts; and scheduling to keep production lines flowing smoothly. Nothing Henry Ford did had not been done to great effect before—in a different context. This takes absolutely nothing away from his achievement. Yet it does mean that your task is easier than you might have thought.

If you have a great idea, and an objective, you can take powerful business genes from elsewhere to implement your vision. Charles Sorensen, who worked with Ford for 40 years,[8] should give hope to us all:

> *"Henry Ford had no ideas on mass production. He wanted to build a lot of autos. He was determined but, like everyone else at that time, he didn't know how ... The essential tools and the final assembly line with its many integrated feeders resulted from an organization which was continually experimenting and improvising to get better production."*

Tweaking and adapting successful ideas proceeds in many different ways. It starts in your mind. What possible variants of a flourishing idea could we dream up? Most of these ideas will be instantly rejected as infeasible, unattractive, or both. Of the few that are feasible and attractive, you will want to float them past other trusted judges. Of the few that survive this process, you will probably make prototypes, in words or models, and test them in front of potential customers. For new products, you may conduct market research, focus groups, or a test market. A new business idea may be tested by exposure to venture capitalists or other providers of funds.

Your chances of success for the new business are dramatically higher if all the following are true:

❖ The idea is a variant of one that has already proved itself successful.

❖ The variant you decide to pursue is one of a very large number of potential variants, and is the survivor of a serious process of business selection, having proved itself superior to all the other variants.

❖ The idea, although a variant of success, is unique—nobody else is pursuing it.

❖ The idea has superior economics to the original idea. Superior economics means a better product or service at the same cost, or a similar product or service at a lower cost. Superior economics always translates into higher return on capital.

❖ The idea fits the 20 percent spikes of you and your partners—it reflects, and can be reinforced by, your own idiosyncracies.

Mutants in consulting and the first business gene: "management consultancy"

To anyone who knows anything about management consulting, the name McKinsey is magic. McKinsey is the most venerable consulting firm and probably still the world's most prestigious and successful firm. McKinsey people always write "Firm" with a capital F when describing themselves.

There was a James O. McKinsey, but the man who put McKinsey on the map was Marvin Bower (born 1903) in the 1940s. His idea was that management consulting could be a profession, just like the law, and that McKinsey could embody the highest professional standards in its dealings with clients.[9]

Today this might seem an odd aspiration: Management consulting is well established and lawyers' ethics are under the microscope. In the 1930s and 1940s, however, management consulting was a fly-by-night and untrusted novelty. In contrast, Bower insisted that McKinsey should put the client's interests ahead of those of the Firm or the individual consultant. Client service, client confidentiality, integrity and responsiveness in dealing with clients: These values were drummed into the McKinsey cadre.

But where did Bower get these ideas? "All" he did was appropriate a successful model from another profession. Every notion he had, every innovation in language and behavior, came from the law. Before Bower, management consultants "worked for" clients. In contrast, lawyers had "client engagements." After Bower, so too did McKinsey.

It was enough. McKinsey became synonymous with high-quality management consulting. The Firm defined its markets as "the board room" and during the 1950s and 1960s had client engagements with most of the world's largest multinational corporations. Each engagement was led by a highly experienced McKinsey officer, typically a man who had seen it all and done it all, whose authority was sealed by gray hair and an impressive collection of hats.

The first mutation: The gene of "strategy consulting"

In 1963, in total obscurity, a new star was born. The star was The Boston Consulting Group (BCG), and the truth is that it happened pretty much by chance. Bruce Doolin Henderson (1915–92) had been fired again. He decided to found his own consulting firm, which initially boasted "one man, one desk, and no secretary."

Bruce's new idea was that BCG should specialize in "strategy" and employ smart business school graduates as its analytical engine room. Before this, strategy did not exist as a recognized discipline. What Bruce did was to take two other thriving, yet much lower-margin products—market research and financial analysis—and fuse them together to make strategy.

Market research was undertaken for marketing departments. Financial analysis served the accounts department. Strategy, Bruce claimed, should be the concern of top management. He went after McKinsey's market, but with a totally new product and a new way of delivering it—via twenty-something business school analysts, not gnarled industry veterans.

Strategy was whatever Bruce and his colleagues said it was. They invented it. They had a loose intellectual monopoly on it. They were the inventors and propagators of "business genes" long before the term had been invented. Their province was ideas for management. Ideas would rule the world. Bruce's obituary in the *Financial Times* said that "few people have had as much impact on international business in the second half of the twentieth century."

The second mutation: The gene of "CEO relationships"

In 1970 a group of senior BCG vice-presidents, led by Bill Bain, left BCG to found Bain & Company. Bain added one crucial new aspect to the DNA invented by BCG: the gene of "CEO relationships."

In 1980 I left BCG to join Bain & Co. What amazed me then, and still amazes me, is how a firm could be so much the same and yet so different. Same product, same type of people, same type of client, same type of analysis, same glitzy offices—but a totally different commercial formula, based around serving the interests of the chief executive officer, and a dramatically different internal style, based on discipline, hierarchy, and teamwork, as opposed to BCG's anarchic, market-based individualism.

There were different results as well. Although BCG's growth and profitability were the envy of most firms, in its first 10 years Bain far surpassed BCG on both dimensions.

The business genes originated by McKinsey had found new vehicles for their replication and expansion: First BCG, then Bain, then a host of other new strategy consulting firms. So powerful were the McKinsey, BCG, and Bain genes that not one of the new firms with these genes failed, a truly remarkable record. The "strategy consulting industry" started by BCG in 1963 has grown since at a compound annual growth rate of about 20 percent: a fantastic record over nearly 40 years.

A third mutation: The genes of "junior staff leverage" and "M&A consulting"

I came pretty late to this honey pot. In 1983 two other Bain partners and I split off to found our own firm, initially called The LEK Partnership (later, LEK Consulting). To start with, we were a slightly pale imitation of

Bain & Co., but we found that we did not have the reputation to insist on Bain-style chief executive relationships. So we had to evolve our own differentiation.

It began with a lucky blunder. The year after we started we had plenty of demand, but not enough staff, so we went on a hiring binge. We tried to hire twenty MBA graduates from the top US schools like Harvard Business School and ten 21-year-old graduates from Oxford and Cambridge. This ratio of two consultants to every associate consultant was the daring level that Bain had reached; hiring the junior people gave extra leverage to the practice.

MBAs, however, saw us as a risky startup. We made many offers but almost nobody accepted.

On the other hand, either because they were more entrepreneurial or more naïve, we were inundated with excellent undergraduate candidates. They didn't seem to care that we were new, and they rated us on the same level as McKinsey, BCG, and Bain—a preposterous idea at the time. We made 30 offers to undergrads. I assured my partners that no more than 10 would accept. In fact, 28 did.

Our staff structure was bizarre. Three partners, four consultants, and nearly thirty associate consultants, none of whom, initially, knew anything about business or strategy. What could we do? We couldn't safely park our associate consultants on client premises. We had to find our young people something to do.

What they could do, very well, was computer analysis of our clients' competitors. Heavy-duty competitive analysis was our firm's 20 percent spike, directly reflecting the superb quantitative skills that Iain Evans brought to our partnership. This was what we trained all our people in, something that was ideally suited to young professionals.

Before long, we stumbled across another way of selling the same work in a different and more lucrative market: the M&A market. More specifically, the "market for clients who wish to make acquisitions in areas they don't fully understand and who are considering target companies that they would like to know a great deal more about." We invented a new product, which later spawned other M&A products—analysis to help win

M&A battles, analysis to defend clients under bid attack, and strategic due diligence for private equity firms and banks backing bids for companies.

It worked like a dream. We grew our staff, revenues, and profits at 100 percent a year throughout the 1980s, and by the time I left in 1989 had over 300 professional staff, with offices throughout the world and some of the highest margins in consulting.

We were extremely fortunate in the genes we inherited and the people who made it happen. We were continuing—at that time unconsciously—the replication and enhancement of powerful business genes. We were following the 80/20 principle: Taking a very successful formula, experimenting with a number of tweaks, discarding most of them, and building on the vital few variants that found a receptive market.

New genes for a Cinderella market

Now a different story, where powerful business genes were imported into a dull market, one written off by most observers. If you are in a flat or failing market, take heart. You can import into it successful ideas from other markets.

In the early 1990s the three-star hotel market in England was in disarray. Many hotels made losses and return on sales rarely rose above 10 percent. All the big hotel companies were going upmarket, to glitzy four- and five-star hotels.

I came to this inauspicious market with all the power of ignorance. I knew nothing about hotels. Indeed, I had used some of the capital from selling my stake in LEK Consulting to buy a hotel at the height of a recent boom, and promptly seen my hotel turn from high profits to alarming losses. Serendipitously, I came across three hotel consultants who said they could raise the profits of hotels. They took my hotel in hand and worked their magic, turning my property back into profit. But by that stage the market for hotel consulting was drying up. Interest rates had peaked, good times were coming back, and the big groups were once again sniffing around to buy badly run hotels.

The hotel consultants had a formula for raising profits of hotels that, they claimed, was valid in good times as well as bad. I provided the capital for the purchase of one hotel, transforming a hotel advisory firm into one that owns and runs hotels. The group, renamed Zoffany Hotels, now has 10 hotels, each with a return on sales in the 30–40 percent range, pretty much the highest in the market. The value of the privately traded shares has increased from £1 to £260 in this time.

The Zoffany formula is the result of testing and adapting a large number of winning ideas from more upmarket hotel groups and from other industries, to arrive at a unique mix of ideas:

❖ Focus on the unfashionable part of the market, namely *three-star* hotels in the centers of medium-sized *provincial towns*, where the target market is junior and middle-level executives.
❖ The hotels must have a high relative share of their local market, that is, there must not be a larger competitor *of the same type* in the vicinity.
❖ A rigorous "private equity" approach to *buying* hotels: Zoffany only buys if they are objectively cheap according to industry benchmarks.
❖ A *flatter* management structure than is traditional in the industry: Zoffany has a very small head office and no regional manager tier. Hotel general managers report directly to one of the two Zoffany partners.
❖ A focus on *bedrooms* rather than other hotel operations such as lounges and dining rooms. Zoffany buys hotels where there is scope to add new bedrooms, because accommodation is by far the most profitable activity in its market.
❖ *Cheap development*—when Zoffany builds new bedrooms it does so at well below the cost for competitors, using local builders supervised by one of the Zoffany directors.

This combination of ideas perfectly matches the skills of Zoffany's two leaders, Niall Caven and Nick Sonley.

How to enlist and mutate great ideas

1 Circle your wagons

Define the domain within which you will enclose your great idea. Do this in two ways. First, think of the type of business you wish to start, and what ideas have previously worked best in that territory.

Complement this by gathering and sorting through some great ideas from other industries. Recall Marvin Bower. None of us would have heard about McKinsey if Marvin had simply taken the best from the consulting industry. Marvin's genius was to think about law firms. What other prosperous industries or firms could you emulate? Think of one that could be applied to your market but on which nobody has yet drawn.

2 Shortlist the vital few ideas

Find complementary ideas that can be combined in novel ways. To qualify, each idea must demonstrate that it is one of the vital few. The firms that embody the idea must be unusually profitable, at least in the area where the idea operates. The idea must demonstrate unusual customer appeal, or elegant economy, or both. It must offer more for less. Strike out anything that is not in the top 20 percent of super-productive ideas.

Whittle away at your shortlist until you have between three and five vital few ideas.

3 Ferment a unique brew

Try combining the ideas until you come up with a unique new business idea that you think will work. In some cases the answer will be obvious. I don't know if Marvin Bower suddenly ran naked out of his bathtub and down the streets of Chicago shouting, "Eureka! Make consulting a profession like the law." Somehow, I doubt it—he wouldn't have forgotten his hat. But he may only have played around with one basic idea.

Or a unique brew may result from no more than two previously separate ingredients, as when Bruce Henderson mated market research with financial analysis.

Still, play the permutations. If you have five ideas and want to look at all possible mixes of any two of them, you will define ten possible new combinations. If you want to combine any three of five ideas, there are another ten possible mixes. Not all of them may be sensible, but not all of them would necessarily be obvious either. Write out the possible combinations.

Don't neglect any dimensions of uniqueness that you can imagine. I can think of six dimensions:

❖ Product.
❖ Service.
❖ Time (to design or deliver a product or service).
❖ Customer.
❖ Geography.
❖ Activity (type and stage of value added, for example design, research, exploration, manufacturing, selling, distribution, or any permutation of these variables).

Arrive at a shortlist of between one and three new great ideas that must define a venture in an exciting and innovative way, and differentiate it from any existing business.

4 Test, Test, Test

Test your shortlist on as many people as possible (exclude competitors and thieves). If one or more ideas survive this process, run or simulate a test market. Try small-scale experiments that will validate or damn your great idea.

5 Confirm the economics of an 80/20 enterprise

Bring together the words and the music (numbers; see Chapter 5) and see if they fit. Work out the numbers for the great idea. Unless the numbers demonstrate very high return on capital and higher margins than in earlier variants of the same idea, your new great idea isn't one!

6 Discover the new 20 percent within the 20 percent

If things don't go as well as you expected, it may be that you have some of the ingredients of a great idea, but that you have either have too many or too few ingredients. Experiment with taking out or adding new variables until the business has the returns that characterize an 80/20 enterprise.

Even if everything goes according to plan, conduct a large number of experiments to vary your successful formula. There is always a new 20 percent of super-successful forces within or adjacent to the successful enterprise. We will return to this point in Chapter 11.

Repeat steps 1–6 until you are confident in the new great idea. Then look for great people and capital to launch it. Then just do it!

The story of Betfair

Stock exchanges have been around for many centuries. So why not a betting exchange? Andrew "Bertie" Black, son of the anti-betting fanatic and Tory MP the late Sir Cyril Black, could see no reason why not. Mr. Black Jr. teamed up with young investment banker Edward Wray to create The Sporting Exchange Limited.

Trading as Betfair, the company allows people to place bets with other individuals, without the intervention of a bookmaker. Typically, a bookie takes a profit margin of 15–20 percent on each event. Betfair's average margin is 1.4 percent, deducted from winning bets, which means that the value for those who bet via an exchange is hugely greater than going to a bookmaker. Not only that—for the first time, an individual like you or me can act as the "layer," specifying a horse, player, or team that we think *won't* win the event, usually a great deal easier than picking the winner.

Betfair's proposition is specifically designed for the serious enthusiast and gambler, where value is of the essence. It makes it possible for skillful individuals to win money at gambling, something previously almost impossible. Not surprisingly the business, launched just two years ago, is proving enormously attractive, with trading volumes already at an annual running rate of nearly £1 billion and rising by more than 20 percent *a month*. I am an investor and outside director, and think it possible that Betfair will be worth several billion dollars within a few years.

Betfair is a brilliant idea, executed with great aplomb. Yet in a sense, it is nothing more than the idea of the stock market, one of the most successful ideas of the last two centuries, translated to the betting market.

What other successful idea is waiting for you to adapt it to another market?

The story of Rachel

What business genes lie behind Rachel's business? As with Zoffany, no individual element is unique, but the combination is the following:

❖ Understanding of her carefully targeted niche markets and the brands that have become synonymous with these markets.

❖ Designs from interesting countries, including Bangladesh, Morocco, and Estonia, using a network of freelancers, often from fashion schools, designing clothes exclusively for Rachel.

❖ Expertise in selling these products within department stores, generating very high margin per square foot.

❖ A relentless focus on return on sales and return on capital, broken down into each element of activity (Rachel's second initial is *M* and the joke within her business is that it stands for "margin").

❖ A merchandising approach that manages the business according to realistic expectations of sale prices, and therefore requires product cost to be low enough to make high net margins. Rachel explains: "Whereas all my competitors assume that they will sell their product at full price, so that write-downs and sell-offs hurt their margins, we assume from the start that we will fail. I manage the business assuming that we will sell only 40 percent of our clothes at full price. Of the rest, we assume 60 percent will be sold at 40 percent off, 33 percent will be sold at clearance prices, and 7 percent will have to be written

off. We can usually do better than this. But what it means is that the
product cost has to be low enough to sustain this mix of margins."

Rachel is a great proponent of variation and improvement. Each season
brings a new range for each brand, with a fresh theme and new clothes
from new designers. Each year has its own new crusade for selling more
to customers and for reducing product cost.

"I'm not talking about overhead reduction." She jabs her finger at me.
"There's a limit to that. It's the cost of goods that has to come down. I
tell my designers each year that the cost price for each type of apparel has
to be such-and-such, which is always lower than the year before. The
designers themselves are involved in cutting the costs, they're not just
airy-fairy fashion artistes. It has to do with the fabric that we choose and
all kinds of things you couldn't imagine. More for less is what you say.
We've been doing it for years."

Notes and references

1 Richard Dawkins (1995) *River Out of Eden*, Weidenfeld & Nicholson,
London.
2 Charles Darwin (1859) *On the Origin of Species by Means of Natural Selection;
Or, the Preservation of the Favoured Races in the Struggle for Life*, John Murray,
London.
3 Since Vilfredo Pareto's discovery that eventually evolved into the 80/20
principle was only made in 1897, Darwin clearly was not aware of the idea
explicitly. One could, however, construct an interesting hypothesis that
Darwin was the real inventor of the 80/20 principle.

What is interesting about eighteenth- and nineteenth-century
thought—as a wonderful illustration of my theme about ideas and the 80/20
principle—is how ideas develop out of other successful ideas. Darwin's theory of natural selection rested on evolutionary ideas common to the early
nineteenth century. What Darwin did was to explain plausibly—and, in ret-
rospect, almost certainly correctly—how evolution took place. To do so, he
appropriated another successful piece of late eighteenth/early nineteenth-
century furniture, the idea of competition. Darwin's idea of the "struggle for

life" was a direct cross of Adam Smith's theories of competition and Thomas Malthus' theory of population growth leading to death through starvation. For more on the origins of Darwin's idea see Richard Koch (2000) *The Power Laws of Business: The Science of Success*, Nicholas Brealey, London, or the American edition, Richard Koch (2001) *The Natural Laws of Business*, Currency Doubleday, New York, Chapters 1–3.

It is also intriguing to note the parallels between the 80/20 principle, natural selection, and Joseph Schumpeter's insight that capitalism (or, as I would prefer, free enterprise) proceeds via "the perennial gale of creative destruction." In remarkably contemporary, even biological, language, Schumpeter described this in 1942:

"The same process of industrial mutation ... that incessantly revolutionizes the economic structure from within, incessantly destroying the old one, incessantly creating a new one. This process of Creative Destruction is the essential fact about capitalism.

"In capitalist reality, as distinguished from its textbook picture, it is not [competition in a static market] which counts but the competition from the new commodity, the new technology, the new source of supply, the new type of organization (the large-scale unit of control for instance)—competition which commands a decisive cost or quality advantage and which strikes not at the margins of the profits and outputs of the existing firms but at their foundations and their very lives...

"In the case of the retail trade the competition that matters arises not from additional shops of the same type, but from the department store, the chain store, the mail-order house and the supermarket."

See Joseph A. Schumpeter (1942) *Capitalism, Socialism and Democracy*, Harper & Row, New York. I quote from the 1962 Harper Torchbook edition, pp. 83–7. It would be very easy to "translate" Schumpeter's ideas into either the process of natural selection described by Darwin or the dynamic 80/20 principle process described in this chapter.

The free market creates new economic forms that start as minority variants and end up destroying most of the existing economy—to be replaced in due course by other minority variants that have extraordinary power. Because Schumpeter grasped the dynamics of private enterprise he was relatively unconcerned about oligopoly. Sooner or later a superior form of enterprise would replace monoliths, so long as the market was left alone to do its work.

4 The inventor of the "gene-based" view of life, the view that genes are more fundamental than species or individuals, is Richard Dawkins, the brilliant Oxford biologist. The best account is still Richard Dawkins (1976, revised edition 1989) *The Selfish Gene*, Oxford University Press, Oxford.

5 This is my theory of "business genes," which derives from Richard Dawkins' concept of "memes." A meme is a unit of cultural transmission, like a book, a play, a song, or an idea. A meme is a human artefact, a form of replication peculiar to humans. Memes operate in a way similar to genes.

6 As Richard Dawkins says, "It is not success that makes good genes. It is good genes that make success." See note 4 above.

7 David Hounshell (1984) *From the American System to Mass Production, 1800–1932: The Development of Manufacturing Technology in the United States*, John Hopkins University Press, Baltimore.

8 Charles E. Sorensen with Samuel T. Williamson (1956) *My Forty Years with Ford*, Norton, New York.

9 Marvin Bower (1966) *The Will to Manage: Corporate Success through Programmed Management*, McGraw-Hill, New York.

5 Enlist the Vital Few Profit Forces

"He that is everywhere is nowhere."

Thomas Fuller (1654–1734)

The 80/20 principle uses numbers to identify the vital few forces that can bring success to you. Just as music arranges sounds in a pleasing sequence and combination, so the numbers tell us when we have arranged business in an economically pleasing sequence and combination.

Few whole businesses are extremely profitable, yet many parts of businesses are. Our task, using the 80/20 principle, is to identify the most profitable parts of businesses, so that we may use similar components as building blocks for our new enterprise.

When 80/20 people target the most profitable markets and the most productive inputs to businesses, and when we produce results that stack up numerically—when cash flow is high relative to investment—then we are making music.

In Chapter 4 we worked down from ideas to help define your new venture. In this chapter, we will work up from numbers, from profitable fragments of businesses, to get clues of what the new venture should do. We will use inductive reasoning: By identifying the vital few profitable forces in numbers, we will have the ingredients of success for a new permutation for an enterprise. Wallow in the numerical detail for a while. Try to define the shape of the new business from the bottom up.

Finding the vital few profit forces

Our challenge is to find the vital few, the minority of forces that create wealth in any arena.

Examine the accounts of any company and you will learn that it earns a certain return, say 15 percent return on capital. That is true, but it is not the whole truth, not the interesting truth. A few small parts of the business may earn 60 or 70 percent return on capital, and other substantial chunks may lose money.

In a good year, the US economy will grow at 3 percent. Yet a few firms will grow at 20, 50, or even 100 percent. In a corporation growing at 20 percent, certain products may more than double their annual sales.

Look around a large office. Everyone may seem to be busy and productive, but a few people will be adding 10 or 20 times more value than the rest.

Reflect on how you spend your time. A few of the things you do, relative to the time they take, will create 10-20 times more wealth than the rest. Several things you do probably destroy wealth.

In thinking about the "raw materials" for a new business—the product and service areas you might enter, the type of customers you might serve, the geographic limits of the business, the ideas, technologies, and business models you might use, the people you will employ and the other partners who are important but will not be employed, the suppliers you will have and what you will ask them to do for you—there are two critical issues:

❖ What is going to create the most wealth for the least effort and capital? *This is the wealth-creating question.*

❖ What are the powerful forces to have on my side? For each type of force (product and service, customer, etc.), which of them produces 80 percent of the result for 20 percent of the resource? Which are the vital few? *This is the 80/20 question.*

Deconstruct reality

The world deals mainly in averages. However, averages mislead. Things that are very different get lumped together. Because most things are like the average, we miss the few that are not at all similar.

Apparently, results are hard to get. A tortuous, complex process seems necessary to grind out results: "blood from a stone." Yet if we look beneath the surface, we see that while most forces are treading water, the vital few really powerful forces are gliding effortlessly toward success. To change the metaphor, "a warm knife through butter."

Whenever we see anything—an industry, a market, a corporation, a technology, a group of people, an idea, a methodology, or any other aspect of business—we shouldn't accept it at face value. Instead, "deconstruct" reality. Look beneath the surface until you find the vital few. Consider how to ride them to success.

In foraging for the vital few, what we are doing is "de-averaging." We are taking apart an average and searching for the few fantastically productive parts of the average: the 20 percent, or 5 percent, or 1 percent that is delivering most of the goods.

What makes a consulting firm super-profitable?

As the co-owner of a consulting firm, this question excited me. How might the 80/20 principle identify the vital few?

My partners had the hypothesis that we should concentrate on large projects. Perhaps large projects were the vital few. This would be true if 80 percent of profits came from large projects comprising only 20 percent of sales revenues.

When I did the analysis, this proved to be half right. Large projects accounted for 21 percent of revenues but a whopping 56 percent of profits. Return on sales for large projects was 46 percent, and for small projects less than 10 percent, so the large projects were more than four times as profitable—certainly well worth knowing.

However, we had not yet found the key 80/20 relationship: There must be more than the difference between large and small clients. So I asked, "What other types of work are super-profitable?" One answer was "old" clients: not client personnel, but clients where we had worked continuously for more than two years. Analysis revealed an 80/20 relationship! Old clients comprised 26 percent of revenues, but a stunning 84 percent of profits. Old clients were the vital few. Their return on sales was 55 percent, whereas for intermediate-length clients (more than six months of continuous work but less than two years) the return on sales was 13 percent, and for new clients it was a loss of 31 percent.

We worked out why. New clients take a lot of work to land them, then to work out what is really happening there and to build credibility through delivering results. At first, all clients are skeptical and price sensitive. In older client relationships, you know the terrain and how to get results, they trust you, and they don't want to get new consultants in, which would be disruptive and incur costs in new learning.

Concentrating on old clients might seem a recipe for stagnation: No new clients, no new fees. But this was conventional thinking. 80/20 thinking finds creative ways to increase the most profitable business. So we reflected: What if the best people in the firm, instead of focusing on new business, worked on generating more from old clients and making all clients "old" clients. Our goal was redefined: Keep existing clients and raise our billings to them.

We had found our vital few: working long term and at high levels for our clients. The vital few became the vital many, with great results. We were highly profitable and doubled in size each year for six years.

What were Filofax's vital few?

Filofax was almost bust when Robin Field and I rescued it in 1990. Robin tells what he found:[1]

> *"While Filofax design and features had remained static, the product line width had expanded beyond all control. The same basic binder was available in a bewildering variety of sizes and a huge assortment of—mainly exotic—skins. Name a creature and Filofax would have ordered several thousand binders made of its hide and proudly placed them in its catalogue and in stock. I don't know what a Karung is, but I inherited an awful lot of its skin in 1990.*
>
> *"Similarly, name a subject: bridge, chess, photography, bird watching, windsurfing, and Filofax would have commissioned several specialist inserts, had tens of thousands of them printed, and put them in inventory...*
>
> *"The result was, of course, not only a huge overhang of worthless stock, not only an administrative burden of vast complexity, but total confusion among our retailers."*

We concentrated on the vital few: the 20 percent of product and the 20 percent of customers that gave us 80 percent of our margin. Within three years, Robin had turned a large loss into a 15 percent net profit, while quadrupling our volume sales. The stock price went from 30p to over 200p.

How to enlist the vital few profit forces

Divide reality into three main categories: employees and partners, customers, and product and service segments. For each, find the vital few profit forces: the 20 percent giving you 80 percent of profits.

Who are the vital few people?

Identify the super-productive and super-cheap employees, and what they have in common.

In my consulting organization this was easy. The people at the bottom of the professional hierarchy were not just the cheapest, they were also the most productive.

Our professional staff split into three broad categories. At the top were the partners. Next came the consultants, typically aged around 30, armed with MBAs and attitude. The bottom layer was comprised of associate consultants or researchers. These were around 21–25 with good undergraduate degrees and spent most of the day manipulating data and conducting analyses on their PCs.

The partners were expensive; since we owned the firm, we preferred it that way. Less gratifying was the cost of the consultants. Nowadays they start at $100,000 and many cost much more. The kids—sorry, associate consultants—were a bargain. They had amazing energy. They often put in 80-90 hours a week. Hour for hour, the associate consultants were cheaper than the secretaries.

In a consulting firm, as with lawyers, you aim to bill all the hours spent on client engagements. The associate consultants were extremely profitable, for two reasons. One, we could bill them out at a higher multiple of salary (based on a standard eight-hour day) than we could other staff —a clear clue that they generated more wealth relative to their cost. And two, they worked more hours. The kids were our vital few.

Most consulting firms bulge in the middle: There are a few partners, a mass of consultants, and a few junior professionals at the bottom. When we found that the associate consultants were our vital few we made them the vital many, constructing for the first time in our industry a genuine pyramid with a larger number of junior staff at the base. The kids became the largest group of professionals. Our profits soared.

Who are the vital few customers?

We saw earlier that in the consulting business the most profitable clients were old clients. This is very often true, whatever the business. That is why firms that retain a higher proportion of their clients have much higher profits.

In a professional services business, owned by its partners, profitability is not the only criterion for selecting clients. The enjoyment and professional satisfaction of the partners and other staff are also important: Professional firms compete for the best staff as well as for clients. A firm of accountants in New Zealand I know grades its clients on the following criteria:

❖ Whether the staff like the client...
❖ and respect the client.
❖ Whether the client respects the staff.
❖ Whether the client doesn't complain about the fees...
❖ and pays on time...
❖ and offers opportunities for growth in billings.

1 Define the vital few super-profitable customers

If you were to start a new venture in any particular area—and you may want to think of several potential areas where you could do this—what type of customers would you want? In defining the vital few most profitable customers, you are bound to gain some valuable clues as to the possible shape of your future venture.

Try to imagine who would comprise the vital few super-profitable customers on the following dimensions:

❖ Size of customer (in revenues to you).
❖ Longevity of customer.
❖ Typical purchase quantity per order (customers taking large deliveries, even if infrequent, are often much more profitable).
❖ Main product or service bought (some products are much more profitable than others).

❖ Breadth of purchases. Those buying only one product are sometimes much more profitable because you get a long run of that product, or because the product itself is lucrative; but sometimes customers buying the whole range are more profitable because they pay top dollar for their less important purchases.

❖ Smart or stupid? Lazy or on the ball? Smart customers are sometimes best because they improve your products, thus keeping you ahead of the competition. But lazy customers are sometimes great because they are not price sensitive. Many banks make all their money out of lazy customers, for example those who keep a great deal of cash on deposit despite low interest rates.

❖ Senior or junior? For products and services sold to other corporations, it is generally true that the most profitable customers are the most senior in the hierarchy. Chief executives are often the best clients.

❖ The personality of the customer is sometimes important. One consulting firm I know deliberately targeted "paranoid" clients because they would buy large amounts of consulting if they thought it gave them security, including security from their colleagues!

❖ For consumer goods, try the usual demographic criteria (such as income level) and lifestyle criteria (such as risk taker versus risk avoider, or technophile versus technophobe). My experience, however, is that such "canned" criteria (those measured by advertising and marketing agencies) rarely correlate with the vital few. The vital few usually cut across canned criteria—what makes them vital is not obvious to marketeers.

One reason the few are so vital is because suppliers are not explicitly targeting them. If the vital few were obvious and assiduously courted by most suppliers, they wouldn't remain super-profitable for very long.

2 Identify the customers with the highest ratio of value to cost

The same product or service may have very different value to different customers. Alternatively, small and inexpensive tweaks of the product or service may enable it to sell to upscale customers and command a much higher price.

One of the most instructive cases is that of strategy consultants Bain & Co. As we saw in Chapter 4, Bain was formed in 1970 when Bill Bain, a senior officer at The Boston Consulting Group, resigned to head his own firm. Bain undertook pretty much exactly the same work as BCG—the product, if you like, was identical—but targeted the product exclusively at the top person in any corporation, the group chief executive officer (CEO), in particular new group CEOs. Instead of selling individual projects to division heads or other senior managers, Bain sold exclusive relationships that encompassed many projects, all sponsored by the CEO.

The Bain consulting program often became the way a new CEO made his mark on the group. Bain projects provided information and insight, which enabled the CEO to make radical changes quickly. Most new CEOs working with Bain were able to impress the financial markets and their shares surged.

The service and the offering were transformed, as was the price. The delivery of the product—the actual process of consulting, the analysis of costs, customers, and competitors—remained unaffected; its unit cost did not rise. Margins and growth did.

From a standing start, Bain became one of the world's top consulting firms, by identifying the customers with the highest ratio of value to cost.

Bain refused to work for the majority of clients that most consulting firms are eager to court; it would not work for finance directors, marketing directors, or even divisional CEOs, however large their companies. A growth strategy that eliminates most potential consulting clients might seem bizarre, but it demonstrates the power of cutting out everything but the vital few forces.

By concentrating on the most profitable and agreeable clients, the New Zealand accounting firm mentioned earlier cut its client base in half. Yet activity levels per retained client doubled and charge-out rates rose by a quarter. Staff morale soared.

It seems perverse to voluntarily chop out half of your clients. Nevertheless, the really profitable forces are so vital that they overwhelm the trivial many.

What are the vital few activities, products and services?

In addition to the vital few customers, identify the vital few things that customers value. Then consider confining your activities to these few things.

In finding the vital few activities, products, and services, there may be clues from the most profitable players. What is it that they do differently?

Imitation is not enough, however. 80/20 people create their own vital few mix, something new and unique. Play around with the following seven generic themes, to mix and match some of them to the area that best fits your 80/20 spike and that you know best.

1 Think small

This is classic segmentation, focusing on only one part of an established market.

The US and European motorcycle markets used to be essentially one big market, dominated by the serious motorcycle manufacturers such as Harley-Davidson, Norton, and Triumph. In the 1960s Honda introduced much smaller motorbikes to the American market, creating an entirely new market and appealing to many people who were new to motor-cycling. BMW later created another segment, with wide, comfortable bikes for broad-bottomed people.

2 Think big

Re-segment, creating a bigger market, either by combining more than one existing product or technology, or by taking a product or technology into new applications. Here are some examples:

❖ US semiconductor maker NEC decided in 1980 to create new segments based on the convergence of computers and telecoms. Within eight years its revenues had increased from $10 billion to $22 billion.
❖ Honda does not base its strategy on conventional market classifications such as motorcycles, lawn mowers, cars, or power generation equipment. It has entered all these markets based on its commitment to have

the world's best small engines. Honda's vital few focus is its unrivaled expertise in small engines—to be more precise, in multilevel cylinder heads with self-adjusting valves.

❖ Bain Capital has become the world's most successful private equity house by enlarging the definition of that market. It not only evaluates deals and finances them, but also devises the strategy for its investee companies and supervises their management. For 15 years Bain Capital has been the most profitable private equity firm in the world, doubling the value of its investments each year.

❖ Home delivery pizza used to be a local market. Expansion was constrained by the limit on how far you could take a pizza and keep it hot. Domino's Pizza created an international business based on a specific business formula, including the use of a proprietary envelope to keep the pizza hot and a network of motivated delivery personnel.

3 Think upmarket

Whenever there is a mass market, there is an opportunity to create a niche serving upscale, rich customers.

Examples include Ferraris, Rolexes, American Express charge cards, private banks, and expensive beer brands.

Toyota, a company with fantastic engineering skills and low-cost production, broke into the luxury car market in 1989 with the launch of its Lexus brand. It provided a splendid product, launched with expensive, effective advertising, but raised the price on the Lexus far above the extra cost it incurred. By 1992 the Lexus brand was small compared to Toyota's total sales—only 2 percent—yet comprised about 30 percent of Toyota's profits.[2]

4 Think mass market

Whenever there is a market largely confined to rich consumers, there is an opportunity to create a mass market by making the product or service much simpler, cheaper, and in higher volumes.

Examples include the Ford Model T, package holidays, budget airlines, and fast-food restaurants.

5 Pursue value innovation: Provide more for less

This is a very fertile category. Provide better value for a new part of the market that you define and create. How? Add and subtract.[3]

Addition is offering some better or extra services, particularly when they can be provided at relatively low cost.

Subtraction means not offering some parts of the traditional product or service package.

The new combination of products and services offers greater value, but only to part of the old market: customers who like the new mix of product offering and price. Change the mix to appeal to a particular group of customers that you define:

❖ Formule 1, a French hotel chain, provides cheap and small but excellent, quiet, and clean hotel rooms with large, comfortable beds. The rooms are modular and mass manufactured, ensuring good sound insulation and low cost. But you won't find lounges, a concierge or room service, or 24-hour reception at Formule 1.

❖ Southwest Airlines offers low fares, very frequent flights between the cities it serves, 10-minute check-in times, and automated ticketing at the gate. It's fast, reliable, and cheap—and very profitable. How come? Southwest doesn't offer many of the expensive services provided by traditional airlines. It doesn't use large airports or long routes, ticket bags through to other destinations, feed you, or offer a choice of cabins. It has a standard fleet of 737s, cutting maintenance costs and delays. It encourages direct payment, cutting out commissions to travel agents and reducing accounts receivable. Southwest appeals to a certain type of traveler who appreciates the trade-offs it makes.

❖ European furniture retailer Ikea sells stylish goods at low prices by making customers, mainly young parents, do the hard work of choosing, paying for, picking up, delivering, and assembling the furniture. In return it offers what they need: not just innovative design and low prices, but also late opening hours, in-store child care, great room displays, and instantly available stock.

❖ Kinepolis, the Belgian movie theater "megaplex," has also developed a business model to appeal to young couples. It is located off the Brussels ring road, with free car parking (an innovation for Europe), 25 screens, unrestricted views, superb sound, and 7,600 wide, comfortable seats with oodles of leg room. Movie-goers enjoy the pick of blockbusters and a radically better cinema experience at a low price. Yet Kinepolis is exceptionally profitable because of low land costs and economies of personnel and overhead, as well as high utilization rates.

6 Use direct distribution channels

Channels requiring real estate, on-site inventory, and personal service are expensive. Direct channels are cheap, and are often the clue to creating a new 80/20 venture.

Dell Computer Corporation innovated in 1984 by selling personal computers direct to consumers, cutting out the dealer network by using mail-order catalogs and taking orders by fax and phone. The catalog offers greater choice than would be available in a typical computer store, but also means great cost savings for Dell because goods move from factories only when there is real end-consumer demand. Lower inventory translates into a 6 percent cost-of-goods advantage for Dell; the problem with computer inventory is particularly acute, given that technology is always advancing and prices continually falling. Dell is able to offer lower prices yet have higher profits than traditional suppliers.[4]

7 Focus on activities with the highest ratio of value to cost

Cherry-pick. Find sweet spots. Identify the part of the value chain—the process of getting a product from conception in research, through to design, development, branding, manufacturing, selling, and physical distribution—that has the highest profitability, and focus exclusively on those very profitable activities.

Large, integrated corporations are wonderfully vulnerable to a new entrant that cherry-picks the sweet spot.

What are the hints for finding sweet spots? Find activities with the greatest customer appeal but requiring little capital. Product design, branding, and direct selling are often sweet spots. Manufacturing, physical distribution, and retailing through a fixed store network are often sour spots.

LEK Consulting specialized in the type of strategic advice that could be delivered by its low-cost analysts, the associate consultants. Our young analysts were not ideally suited to talking to senior client personnel, but were dab hands at gathering data on markets and competitors.

We soon realized that our young analysts were also ideally suited to gathering data on potential acquisitions, and before long we had developed specialist expertise in assessing M&A (mergers and acquisitions) opportunities. Because M&A work was dear to the hearts of chief executives, and because the expenses for completed acquisitions did not have to be charged to the profit and loss statement, it was very price-insensitive work. Hence our dream formula: very high prices, very low costs, and fabulous margins.

Other examples include Microsoft, which only works in the most profitable layer in the computer industry, the design of the operating system, or Nike, which designs and brands its athletic footwear, contracting out capital-intensive and low-return activities like manufacturing and retailing.

The story of Rachel

Rachel's womenswear business is highly profitable because of its vital few activities. Its forte is product design, merchandising, and concession retailing within department stores. Done well, these are activities that generate high returns and growth, and require relatively little capital. The trivial many avoided by Rachel's business include manufacturing, warehousing, and the ownership of retail premises.

Rachel's focus on its vital few activities leads naturally to a focus on the vital few people, customers, and products. The most valued and highest-paid people in Rachel's team are all directly involved with product design and selection, selling, marketing, and contact with customers. The products have been grouped into three areas, each with their own brand, and each targeted at well-defined, specific customer groups, such as "career women aged 25–45" or "women shorter than 5 ft 5 in."

The proof that Rachel really is focused on the vital few forces comes from the numbers. Whereas most businesses in her industry make 0–15 percent return on capital, she makes 50–65 percent. Whereas the trivial many have flat or nearly flat profits of 0–5 percent a year, Rachel has taken a business making $2 million profit eight years ago to one making $30 million today.

In making the shortlist for the vital few ingredients for your own business, add this as a final check: Will your new venture be unusually profitable and able to grow unusually fast? Unless you are confident of this, and know why, you can't be sure that yours will be one of the vital few new enterprises.

Combine the top-down and bottom-up views of your new venture

Your bottom-up view of your potential new venture can now be compared to your top-down view derived from Chapter 4.

First, take your conclusions from this chapter, based on the profitable bits of your market, and try to express in words the idea behind your putative new enterprise.

To take the consulting industry example, we identified in this chapter these super-profitable bits:

❖ Old clients, those for whom the firm had been working for at least two years.
❖ New chief executives as clients.
❖ Junior consultants and a bottom-heavy staff structure with a preponderance of kids.
❖ An exclusive focus on a new division of product, business strategy.

Now, take your ideas from Chapter 4—possible new businesses expressed as ideas—and try to combine that with the view from this chapter.

To stick with the consulting example, what we learned in Chapter 4 was that the following super-profitable consulting ideas had evolved:

❖ Consulting as professional engagements serving the board of directors.
❖ The definition of strategy consulting as a new product.
❖ The idea of strategy consulting as a process of CEO relationships.
❖ The use of maximum junior staff leverage.
❖ A new division of strategy consulting, on mergers and acquisitions.

If we were thinking of starting a new consulting business, we should be pleased by the overlap between the top-down and bottom-up views. Either would have put us on the right track—but a synthesis of the two views would put us in the best position.

The bottom-up view of profitable bits stresses the importance of long-standing clients and hence of selecting only clients with the potential for long-term work, and of converting existing projects into new projects with the same client. We would have missed this if we had merely had a top-down view.

The top-down view stresses the importance of innovating a new division of consulting. Like the bottom-up view, it shows that the place to be is the boardroom, that the client you want is a new chief executive, and that the product you sell should be some variant of strategy consulting. What the top-down view of business as ideas demonstrates is that we need our own innovation—in terms of product, client, staff structure, and/or process—to build on and extend the successes of the past.

If we were starting a new consulting business, therefore, we would probably take all the successful ideas and profitable components from the past and present, but add a new product line or process. We could brainstorm several candidates for the missing ingredient and then ask:

❖ How would we define the idea in words, so that it would be a direct descendant of current successes yet have its own unique niche?

❖ If we were then to undertake a bottom–up analysis, would the new bit be unusually profitable? Could we be sure that the total business would be too?

As it happens, describing this process for you has led me to a fantastic idea for a new type of consulting business—but I'm not telling you what it is!

Is your potential new business one that superbly fits your 20 percent spike?

Now combine your findings from Chapters 4 and 5 with those from Chapter 3. If you're not the best person in the world to create the new business, you'd better change the business definition, or find a partner with whom the fit between business idea and personal mission is terrific.

However, don't close off your options yet. There is one more dimension of business to consider before crystallizing your choice of domain: the dimension of time. Chapter 6 outlines what we get when we mix Vilfredo Pareto with Albert Einstein.

Notes and references

1   Robin Field (1995) "Branded consumer products," in James Morton (1995) *The Financial Times Global Guide to Investing: The Secrets of the World's Leading Investment Gurus*, Financial Times Prentice Hall, London, pp. 469–73.

2   See W. Chan Kim and Renée Mauborgne (1999) "Creating new market space," *Harvard Business Review*, January–February.

3   See the extremely useful article: W. Chan Kim and Renée Mauborgne (1997) "Value innovation: The strategic logic of high growth," *Harvard Business Review*, January–February.

4   The calculation that Dell has a 6 percent cost of goods advantage comes from Deutsche Morgan Grenfell Technology Group (1997) *The PC Industry*, Deutsche Morgan Grenfell.

6 *Enlist Einstein*

"For tribal man space was the uncontrollable mystery. For technological man it is time that occupies the same role."

Marshall McLuhan

Albert Einstein, a poor clerk in the Swiss patent office at the start of the twentieth century, used to ride the tram every day up the Kramgasse in Berne. He imagined that he was traveling toward the clock tower at the speed of light. Given that the light rays reflecting his image were zooming at the same speed, would he be able to see himself in the driver's mirror?

Eventually, he realized that nothing in nature happens instantly, at precisely the same time. The speed of light is absolute, but time and space are relative. Views of time and space are affected by each other.

Einstein changed our view of the physical world. There used to be three dimensions of space. Einstein's general theory of relativity argued in 1916 that time is not independent of space. Time can be warped by gravity. Time is just like a fourth spatial dimension. Instead of the three dimensions of space, there are four dimensions of the space–time continuum, time being the fourth.

The relativity theory totally subverts the ideas of "space" and "time." According to Einstein, space and time are not realities of nature. Instead, they are a simple psychological effect, a product of the material world. As Einstein said, "It was formerly believed that if all material things disappeared out of the universe, time and space would be left. According to the relativity theory, however, time and space disappear together with the things." Yikes!

If you find all this perplexing, join the club. With difficulty, scientists have caught up with Einstein and proved him right in all essentials. Yet business and other creative endeavors have not reached this level. We have a pre-Einsteinian view of time as a separate dimension of activity. This gives 80/20 people an enormous opportunity.[1]

Two ways time relativity could help you define your new venture

Here are two themes that could help you twist your business idea into a unique shape. First, in business as in the rest of life, *time is not "other."* It is part of the warp and woof of the physical things we make and provide to customers. It is part of our products, part of our services, part of our raw material, part of our output.

Therefore, we should not think of what we do for customers as separate from the time we take to do it. *We should not think of products or services on the one hand, and time on the other. We should think of "product-time" and "service-time."* Time is part of what we add or subtract.

Providing an existing product or service in a much faster way could change its economics and offer you a terrific new business idea.

Secondly, in thinking about time as a separate dimension of our lives, we rapidly slide into the view that time is finite and short, that it is in some sense our enemy, or at least a commodity in extremely short supply. Yet time is none of these things. Time is a dimension of our life and experience. Time is an integral part of what we do and who we are. Time is a dimension exactly like space, a place where we can express ourselves and create things of value to others, and therefore to ourselves.

For those of us not mired in poverty or prison, it would be nonsense to say, "I don't have enough physical room to express myself; there is not enough space in my life." But people often do say, "I don't have enough time to express myself; I don't have enough time to do what I want." Although it sounds more plausible, it is equal nonsense.

Combining Einstein with Pareto, we discover that *if 80 percent of the wealth (or anything else desirable) we create happens in less than 20 percent of the time available, then there is no shortage of time.* For individuals and business ventures alike, there is no shortage of time. We use our time most productively for only a small part of our existence. Most of what we do doesn't really matter. The problem is our trivial use of time, not time itself. More fundamentally, our problem is triviality itself: not fulfilling our potential, or anywhere close to it.

It follows that any venture or person could achieve much more while using much less time. The 80/20 principle suggests that you could work a two-day week and still achieve 60 percent more than you do now.

Furthermore, *what we are best at, the activities that make the very best use of our time, must define our new business and make it unique.* Einstein reinforces the idea of the 20 percent spike and redefines the spike in terms of time—the greatest value that we add in the smallest slivers of our time.

How to enlist Einstein

Think product-time, think service-time

1 Compress the time taken to deliver to customers

A product or service delivered in half the time, or double the time, is not the same product or service. Delivering in less time will usually both cut costs and please customers—a double win that should be reflected in higher margins.

It is possible that insight along these lines will lead you to a different shape of business, a much more effective one than currently exists. If so, celebrate! The business gene of time revolution has shown you the shape of your future. If the ideas below do not lead to a radical new plan, or at least a radical new hypothesis to be tested, you have not used them properly.

❖ For any business you are in or might enter, identify the 20 percent of activities that take 80 percent of the time and the 20 percent that comprise 80 percent of your total cost (they are often the same).

❖ Work out what you would need to do to cut the time taken in half. Decide if it is worthwhile and where it would lead.

❖ Then repeat the exercise (at least in your head) another three times. You will have cut the time four times, which means it will now be just over 6 percent of what it used to be. This 16 times improvement is what we should expect with the 80/20 principle (I will explain why in the next chapter).

❖ Work out if, as a result of these changes, costs would be significantly lower or customer satisfaction higher. If so, make the changes. Make them hard for competitors to copy.

Self-service is often the way; a very old idea, which still has terrific innovative power. The essence of self-service is that you delegate certain tasks—preferably the most expensive or time-consuming ones—to the customer. Think how long it would take and how much it would cost to pick, pack, and deliver a weekly order of groceries—as internet grocers are discovering. In this case the internet slows things down.

Savvy car makers and video game providers are involving customers in the design and testing of new products. ATMs enable customers to avoid lines, providing cash and other services much more quickly and much more cheaply than in traditional bank branches. Fast-food chains co-opt the customer into replacing waiters and bus boys. Smart consulting firms co-opt client personnel (but please—only the really bright ones!) on to projects; this not only lowers costs, but also leaves the organization better equipped for the future.

Many retailers now provide customers with computer terminals so that they can find and order products without tying up sales people. Not all types of direct retailing—using phone, fax, the internet, and catalogs—

speed up service delivery and cuts cost, but many do.

An intriguing and very creative example of self-service is a new form of gambling that does away with the bookmaker. As mentioned in Chapter 4 I am an investor in and director of Betfair, which provides a person-to-person betting exchange, a wagering version of the stock exchange. The betting exchange enables customers either to take the traditional role of better or punter, or (this is the innovation) to take the role of the layer, the bookmaker. For the first time, punters are enabled to say which horse (or football team, or dog, or golfer) will not win a contest; if they are right they win, without having to find the contest winner themselves.

A pool of betting liquidity is created that increases the options for punters, yet also cuts costs. Betfair operates on a 1.4 percent margin, compared to the 15–20 percent gouged out by traditional bookmakers.

The extent of self-service activity is only constrained by imagination. What might a self-service revolution in your arena lead to?

Time may be compressed in many other ways. I spent two decades in consulting. When I started, a typical project took nine months. When I hung up my consulting boots, it took three months.

I'm still not sure how we saved all this time. Technology and the easier availability of financial data certainly helped. More important were planning techniques that focused consultants on the key issues and reduced the huge amount of time "wasted" on a project—work that went down dead alleys and was never relevant to the final presentation shown to clients. More fundamental still were competition and the increasing willingness of consultants to "turn on a dime" for clients.

Or take Belgo, a restaurant chain started in London in 1992 with my backing. It became a succesful chain of glitzy *moules-frites* emporia modeled on a monastery dining hall, complete with waiters dressed as monks and 200 different Belgian beers from obscure monasteries.

Belgo offered a fun meal in an expensively designed setting at a bargain price: "A £40-a-head experience at a £20-a-head price" was how one of my partners described it. It became very popular and when we sold out on the stock market we made 20 times our original capital.

How could Belgo offer great value yet also be such a profitable venture? It was down to time compression. The Belgo system relied on turning the tables very quickly. Most restaurants have one or two sittings a night, but Belgo often achieved seven or eight. I joked to my partners that we appeared to own a fast-food restaurant (they were not amused, since they took the quality of the food very seriously).

Restaurants in central locations have horrific fixed costs: rent, depreciation, and large chunks of labor cost too. *Many costs are related to time, not to volume.* Squeeze extra revenue out of a given site in a given time, and it drops straight to the bottom line.

In compressing time, Belgo violates many holy cows. Instead of being parsimonious with staff, it floods the place with waiters; more monks per square foot than you'd find in a teeming monastery. Instead of allowing diners to stay as long as they want, customers booking tables are told that they have a 90-minute time slot, which encourages timely arrival.

Belgo provides extraordinarily prompt service. Drink orders are taken within one minute of customers arriving, food orders within three minutes, and the food comes within five minutes of ordering. A customized, automated ordering process and an open-plan kitchen run like clockwork support this delivery. Bills are presented with the last course, or within 15 minutes of the scheduled exit time. Credit cards are processed within a minute of being offered.

Belgo is a just-in-time factory. Many food critics, and some first-time customers, hate it. But it also has many loyal customers who come every week.

2 Plan to cut time

❖ Draw up a physical map or plan of the *flow of activities* necessary to deliver products and service to customers *measured against time*.

❖ Put a box around each activity where the business does something to add value, ensuring that they are placed in sequence. Connect the boxes with arrows.

❖ Against each box put the time taken for each activity. Then put the time typically taken between the boxes, next to the arrows connecting them. Add up the total "box" time and the total "arrow" time.

There are two ways of speeding up. One is to cut the time taken *in the boxes*, to speed up the actual activities provided. The other is to cut the time *between the boxes*.

Typically, more time is taken between the boxes than within them. In other words, firms take more time not doing anything than they do when doing something. "Downtime" may be much greater than "uptime." A study by The Boston Consulting Group found that "typically, less than ten percent of the total time devoted to any work in an organization is truly value-added. The rest is wasted because of unnecessary steps or unbalanced operations."[2]

At Belgo, the process of taking orders (time within the box) could be speeded up only by combining activities, such as showing patrons to their seats and then *immediately* taking their drinks order. But much more important was compressing the time between this "box" and the next one, which was taking the food order. Instead of the standard restaurant time of 10–15 minutes, Belgo reduced it to 2–3 minutes.

In consulting, the best way to compress time is *extensive upfront planning*. One terrific tool was the blank slide presentation, a guess at the start of a project as to what our final presentation would look like. As the work progressed, we either filled in each previously blank slide, or discarded it as irrelevant and substituted another blank slide. This mechanistic exercise, oddly enough, stimulated rather than restricted creativity. It forced us to keep thinking about what the answer might be.

We discovered that less time there was, the more important and urgent it was to start with the plan, and the greater the percentage of time necessary to plan before acting.

Can you use time relativity to refine your business idea and make your prospective venture more distinctive?

Time is subject to the 80/20 principle: Trigger a time revolution

80/20 people are at the heart of their ventures. Equally, the new venture must be at the heart of the 80/20 person. The enterprise must reflect the individual skills and ambitions of the founders, what you are uniquely good at.

1 Identify your most valuable activities

For creative tasks, a small portion of time nearly always leads to most of the value created—for instance, the flash of insight that leads to a new scientific theory, or the idea for a new business.

If we had even a minor flash of insight once a month, we might multiply the wealth we create in that month many times over. It is worth thinking about how to stimulate such insights. How did earlier insights arise? In the office? Over lunch? Walking in the woods? In conversation with a particular person? Talking to customers? Playing golf? Whatever you were doing before, try spending more time on it and see if new insights arise.

By definition, rare flashes of insight cannot fill much of our time. It therefore becomes important to identify, for more routine uses of our time, what are the few most valuable activities.

Think of a week, five days of work. If the 80/20 principle applies, work taking no more than eight hours—20 percent—generates 80 percent of the value. If you can isolate these high-value activities and spend another day on them, without diminishing returns, two days should give you 160 percent of the previous value. In theory, two days' work could be worth 60 percent more than five days' work currently.

Another choice would be to work five days, two on high-value activities and three on low-value ones. The numbers suggest that this would give you 175 percent of today's value.

A final benchmark would be to work five days on high-value activity, for 400 percent of the value.

The catch is that you have to eliminate the low-value uses of your time. You have to stop these activities altogether, or get someone else to do them.

2 Link your high-value activities to your choice of new venture

More important than numbers is the *identity* of your exceptionally wealth-creating activities, and their *relationship to your potential new venture*.

Is your 20 percent spike—your unique, wealth-creating abilities—congruent with the enterprise you are about to create? The match is more crucial than you might imagine.

In Chapter 4 I introduced Zoffany, my hotel business, and its unique mix of business ideas. The Zoffany formula is derived from its two leaders' 20 percent spikes. Niall Caven is a former investment banker who treats hotel acquisitions in the same way a private equity person would: Each new hotel must generate a high internal rate of return, which depends heavily on its initial purchase price. The development plan, which usually means building more bedrooms, must also show a very high rate of return too; the extent of development is driven by the numbers.

In contrast, Nick Sonley, the other Zoffany entrepreneur, is a brilliant hotelier whose is best at coaching general managers and getting them to take responsibility for looking after guests and for maximizing the profitability of their hotels. He is also a dab hand at designing and executing first-rate hotel improvements and extensions at low cost, by carefully selecting and supervising local builders.

In (useful) management jargon, Zoffany's core competencies match those of its two 80/20 people. We try hard to ensure that Niall and Nick spend most of their time on the vital few things at which each is best. But in a way time allocation is secondary. What is of primary importance is that we have crafted Zoffany's strategy around their most vital uses of time. What is unique and valuable about Zoffany as a business system is what is unique and valuable about its leaders.

Belgo was the same. It also had two founders, Denis Blais and André Plisnier. Denis was passionate about design and created the unique Belgo look: the illusion of the monastery eating hall. Denis and André were both wild enthusiasts for Belgian food and particularly high-quality traditional, "peasant" food. André was an experienced bar and restaurant manager who understood the link between speed and profitability; he created the Belgo "factory" mentality and procedures. Although running a restaurant has many activities and in practice they could not confine their activities, at least in the early days, to the high-value ones, what was key about their high-value activities was that these defined Belgo. Their unique and high-value skills made Belgo unique and high value.

In defining your own high-value activities, and those of your part-ners—the things you do that create most wealth, or that could do so—you are not only working out how to spend your time. More vitally, you are devising a blueprint for your new venture. What makes you and your partners unique wealth creators will also be what makes your business unique and super-successful.

The story of Rachel

Rachel always seems relaxed. I ask what her most valuable activities are. She immediately replies, "Design, margin management, marketing, and selecting my top team. I know what will work for each of my customer groups, which product will go with each brand. Because the team is so good, I have an easy time."

"Why do you say 'selecting' your team, not 'managing' or 'leading'?"

"Selecting, yes," she explains, "leading, yes, I suppose so; managing no. They manage themselves. Leading means pointing in the right direction, but the ideas that drive us forward come from all members of the team, it's a collective thing. Look, the really valuable things we do are our ideas—ideas for new products, ideas for improved selling, ideas for lower-cost products, ways to manage our margins even better. I have ideas but so do Helena, and Georgina, and Bill, and many others. What I do is create the environment that brings forth masses of new ideas, and that then sorts the wheat from the chaff. If we agonize over a decision, I know we should reject the idea. The great ideas are always the easy ones, the ones that arise spontaneously, when we all say 'yes' right away."

Do you know what your new venture is yet?

Time is a dimension of the universe, intimately related to the dimensions of space, not something that is outside them or separate from them.

Time is a dimension of business, intimately related to the products and services we offer and to their economics, not something that is outside them or separate from them.

Time is a dimension of ourselves, intimately related to the wealth we create and the unique attributes we have. Time is not outside us. Time is part of the 80/20 person's toolkit. What we learn faster than others and replicate faster than others is also what we are better at than others.

The ability to be super-productive in product-time, service-time, and entrepreneur-time is the basis of a superior business system. Speed and value are one dimension, not two. Speed itself, speed alone, is often a good proxy for value. What defines the value is not parsimony with time but the ability to impress so quickly. What underpins the value is the quality of the skill. Speed is more the result than the cause of the value, but even this is an imperfect expression, because it breaks apart "speed" and "value."

What we choose as our new venture must express our unique ability to create value, and that of our partners. The unique ability of individuals and of the businesses they create should be measured along the single dimension of time-value. Select your new venture by identifying a new business system that can offer a unique and superior package of time-value, one that nobody else could create.

Have Chapters 3–6 led you to a decision on which new venture to try? Chapters 7–10 will help you get started. It's easier than you may think!

Notes and references

1 My focus here has been on how Einstein's theories might be used by entrepreneurs, and in particular how the business gene of time revolution can guide us toward new, unique, valuable businesses. For a fuller account see Chapter 7, "On Relativity," in Richard Koch (2000) *The Power Laws of Business*, Nicholas Brealey, London, or the American edition, Richard Koch (2001) *The Natural Laws of Business*, Currency Doubleday, New York.

2 Mark F. Blaxill and Thomas M. Hout (1987) "Make decisions like a fighter pilot," in Carl W. Stern and George Stalk Jr. (1998) *Perspectives on Strategy*, John Wiley, New York, p. 165.

7 *Enlist Great Individuals*

"If I have seen further, it is by standing on the shoulders of giants."
Sir Isaac Newton

Every venture capitalist knows that there is nothing more important in a new or young business than its people. That's all very well in practice, but how does it work in theory?

The 80/20 principle tells us that there is an enormous difference between the few, best performers and the rest—that fewer than 20 percent of any peer group will typically achieve 80 percent of its results.

Is this right? Does it fit with what we know about people and business success? And, whether it is right or wrong, what are the practical implications of an empirically derived theory that nearly everyone is ignoring?

This chapter can promise you some truly astounding conclusions, both thought and profit provoking.

Mathematics to blow your mind

How much better, in terms of adding value, would you expect the best people to be compared to the rest? 50 percent better? Twice as valuable?

Four times? If someone were twice or four times as valuable, it would clearly be worth paying a large premium to secure their services.

Yet the 80/20 principle suggests that the best 20 percent of any peer group is likely to be at least 16 times as valuable as the other 80 percent.[1] Why 16 times? Let's do a bit of math.

If the most productive 20 percent produce 80 percent of the value, and there are 100 people in the relevant population, then one of the 20 most productive will produce, on average, 4 percent of the total (if 20 produce 80, then 1 produces 80 divided by 20 = 4). Now, if the 80 percent of less productive people produce in total 20 percent, one of them will produce just 0.25 units: 80 produce 20, 1 produces 20 divided by 80 = 1/4.

So the ratio of productivity for the top 20 percent compared to the bottom 80 percent is 4 divided by 1/4 = 16 times.

This can be expressed as follows:

Vital group (20%) $\dfrac{80\% \text{ results}}{20\% \text{ people}} = 4.00$

Trivial group (80%) $\dfrac{20\% \text{ results}}{80\% \text{ people}} = 0.25$

Ratio of vital group to trivial group $= \dfrac{4.00}{0.25} = 16$

Is a difference of 16 times credible?

Differences in measurable intelligence follow a bell curve, not an 80/20 distribution. The top 20 percent of intelligent people are not twice as intelligent as the rest, let alone 16 times brighter. So does this mean that the 80/20 principle is not applicable to people?

Yes and no. Clearly, the 80/20 principle does not apply to intelligence, and therefore not to talent, which is a form of intelligence. However, those of us interested in success and the creation of wealth and wellbeing —in economics rather than psychology—should not be interested in talent *per se*. Talent is a wonderful thing, but if it does not lead to the creation of wealth and wellbeing it is not what we are after.

If we are interested in economics, in success, then the 80/20 principle —with its queer, counter-intuitive, often offensive, and even outrageous results—is what works. The 80/20 principle came out of academic study of economics. The principle arose not because economists wanted it to apply, not because it formed some convenient bridge in their theory, but because it was self-evidently there, observable in so many economic phenomena.

As economist Josef Steindl remarked: "For a very long time, the Pareto law [the 80/20 principle] has lumbered the economic scene like an erratic block on the landscape, an empirical law which nobody can explain."[2]

Vilfredo Pareto's original discovery, which led to the 80/20 principle, was based on observations of incomes and wealth over many time periods and many countries. It was the consistency of observation that led him to the alegbra behind the principle.[3]

A century of egalitarian tax policies has not been able to overturn the 80/20 principle's sway over income distributions. The top 10 percent of the world's population receive 70 percent of its total income and produce 70 percent of its goods and services.[4] In the US, the top 5 percent own as much market wealth as the bottom 60 percent.[5] The wealthiest 20 percent of Americans own 83.9 percent of the country's wealth.[6]

The increasing operation of the 80/20 principle in relation to superstars in the professions and in the entertainment and sports industries, at the relative expense of less successful professionals and of corporations, is evidence of the tenacity of the 80/20 principle specifically in relation to people at work.[7]

Koch's Law of Individual Wealth Creation

So how do we reconcile psychology and economics, the bell curve and the 80/20 distribution? Both arose empirically; both are well proven.

The answer is crystal clear. *The bell curve and the 80/20 principle refer to different things. The bell curve refers to intelligence, to talent; and the 80/20 principle refers to the capacity of individuals to generate wealth and wellbeing.*
Two insights follow:

❖ Talent is not enough. Talent is useless if it doesn't create wealth or wellbeing. *We should therefore ask what converts talent to wealth making.* We must understand this miraculous alchemy.

❖ Contrary to our expectations, and even perhaps to our sense of what is right and proper, the 80/20 principle does refer to the wealth-creating power of individuals. The mathematics of the 80/20 principle apply. *The wealth creators do create at least 16 times more than the rest of the population.*

Michael Jordan is not 16 times more intelligent than other players. He is not even 16 times better on the field. Yet his ability to create wealth is well in excess of 16 times other players'.

In translating talent into wealth creation, in converting psychology into economics, there is a process of economic leverage. Small differences in talent become multiplied into large differences in wealth-creating capacity.

Hence we arrive at Koch's Law of Individual Wealth Creation:

$$\text{Wealth} = (\text{Talent}) \times (\text{Wealth Creation Multiple})$$

Of these two variables, the wealth creation multiple is the more important. This must be true, given that it clearly varies more than talent does.

What is the wealth creation multiple?

We're talking about our friends from Chapter 4, powerful business genes. These are ideas and vehicles that constitute vital packets of economic power, that convert a level playing field into a Michael Jordan playing field, a mere stadium into a Michael Jackson concert, a book that has the same mix of intelligence and wit as many others into a bestseller.

We can thus restate my Law of Individual Wealth Creation as follows:

$$\text{Wealth} = (\text{Talent}) \times (\text{Business Genes})$$

We know that intelligence does not translate into wealth. Were it otherwise, college professors would all be millionaires. It has often been a mystery why certain business folks become so wealthy, when they're palpably not more intelligent than their peers. Nor can it be explained by hard work: Many people work hard and never become rich. Nor, although luck plays a large part, can it be explained purely by luck. Luck, or chance, are words given to something that we cannot explain or influence.

The answer lies in powerful business genes. Although we often, perhaps usually, stumble across these by luck, there is a crucial difference between the super-successful and the rest. Whether intuitively or deliberately, successful people latch on to powerful business genes.

In the past, this may have been largely intuitive. Now, by decoding the science of success, we can engineer the process more deliberately.

Why do intelligent college graduates, who become English literature professors, make much less—easily 16 times less over a lifetime—than their peers who are no more intelligent, but who take jobs in investment banking or in venture capital? The explanation is simple: Investment banking and venture capital are more powerful business genes.

Some business genes are more powerful than others. Which ones? The ones that have a higher wealth creation multiple. Before long, we should be able to study and quantify these objectively.[8]

How to turn talent into wealth

Talent turns into wealth when brought into contact with powerful business genes and when those genes can use the talent for their purposes.

Which is the better bargain: talent or mediocrity? Let's run some numbers.

Assume that the talented minority of a peer group have a skill quotient of 120, and the mediocre majority one of 80. To attract the talented, assume we have to pay not 50 percent more, which would be the "fair" reflection of their worth, but 70 percent more. We must also assume that the talented person and the mediocre person are equally motivated.

To some extent, motivation and talent trade off against each other. Nevertheless, it is a reasonable assumption that you are only going to hire highly motivated people in any case. Incidentally, many mediocre people are highly motivated, which makes it difficult sometimes to spot their mediocrity. It is easier to notice and screen out talented people whose interest in your business is skin deep.

On the face of it, under these conditions, buying talent is a mug's game. Talent appears over-priced.

But remember Koch's Law of Individual Wealth Creation. There is another variable here: the business genes used to convert talent into wealth. True, this applies to both talent and mediocrity. Yet is it reasonable to assume that both talent and mediocrity will make equal use of the powerful business gene? Will both groups milk it for all it is worth? Or will the talented group be better placed to grasp the essence of the powerful business gene? Will they make 10 times the use of it that the mediocre group does? Put another way, will the business gene be able to make 10 times better use of a talented person than a mediocre person?

If so, the results would be as follows:

$$\text{Value of mediocre individual} = 80 \times 10 = 80$$
$$\text{Value of talented individual} = 120 \times 100 = 1{,}200$$

In this case, the talented individual will produce output worth 15 times (1,200/80) that of the mediocre individual, despite being only half as much again more intelligent.

Is this credible? Possibly. I have chosen the "10 times" factor—the use that the talented person makes of a powerful business gene—quite arbitrarily. You may or may not find this plausible.

Note this, however. The calculation above says that a talented individual may produce 15 times more value than someone mediocre. This is close to the 16 times factor implied by the 80/20 principle. Although my reasoning is circular, something like this relationship must apply if we believe that the 80/20 principle applies to the wealth-creating capacity of individuals. And since *this* is well verified, the only thing that can be wrong about my calculation is the relative weights attached to talent and to the *x* factor (which I say comprises business genes).

Either you have to believe that the difference between the intrinsic talent of individuals is greater than I imply—which psychology and common sense tell us it is not—or you have to believe that the difference in the use of business genes is roughly the multiple of 10 that I take.

Of course, this multiple of 10 only applies to an *average* of powerful business genes. In some cases the business genes may not be that powerful, and only give a multiple of, say, 5. At the tail of the distribution the multiplying power of the business gene may be very high indeed, in the hundreds or thousands in extreme cases.

Even if Einstein had an IQ of 200 or 300, the business genes that he played with—the scientific ideas that were the raw material of relativity theory—must have been extraordinarily powerful, way above the average for powerful business genes. The concept of genius alone, that some human beings are very much more intelligent than others, cannot explain the astronomical power of the results that a genius produces. The explanation must lie in leverage. Genius, whether in science or business, lies in *finding and exploiting* powerful business genes. Differences in intelligence become multiplied in their effects.

How to enlist great individuals

1 Practical implications of the Law of Individual Wealth Creation

Hiring talent is a much better deal than hiring mediocrity. In the example I started with, talent that was intrinsically 50 percent better than its peer group was paid 70 percent more. In the calculation we have just done, talent was assumed to produce 15 times the value.

Assume that a mediocre person costs 50 units and a talented person 85 units (70 percent more).

The return on a mediocre individual = 80/50 = 1.6

The return on a talented individual = 1,200/70 = 17.1, that is, more than 10 times the return on the mediocre person.

Talent only turns into wealth creation by the application of powerful business genes. To some extent, new talent itself drives this process. But to a much larger extent, new talent is the beneficiary of business genes, and the process of exploiting them to produce valuable results that has already been worked out by an earlier generation of talented wealth creators—and is already crystallized within a particular industry, corporation, or team.

This explains why, to begin with, talent is not able to command its output value. In an important sense, talent does not, initially, deserve its output value. The value derives from the interaction of the talent with powerful business genes that are readily available within the industry and corporation. The business genes are more important than the talent. Hence talent can be paid more than it deserves (in my example above, a 70 percent premium in pay for a 50 percent difference in intrinsic ability) and yet less than the wealth it can, within the right business environment, create. This is a good deal for all concerned.

Individuals who are employees and who work effectively with powerful business genes may be able to parlay those ideas, with some individualistic tweaking, into a successful new venture—becoming 80/20 people.

2 Exploit the theory of wealth/talent arbitrage

Talent is not difficult to spot. Grab it before your competitors for talent do so, and convert it into wealth-creating capacity as quickly and fully as possible. Recruit the type of talent that is most likely to make the leap to wealth creation quickly.

Talent becomes wealth-creating capacity when it fuses with powerful business genes. To start with, talent has little value. But before long, talent has considerable or great value, independent of its employer. Talent accumulates value as it assimilates and becomes useful to powerful business genes. Exceptional wealth creators become adept at importing all the valuable business genes used by their employers, and more besides.

In truth, this is not just a matter of pure or general talent. It is a matter of visceral motivation combined with the only type of talent that matters: having instincts for spotting the vital few business genes and knowing how to use them to the hilt. In my experience, however, it is extremely difficult to assess relative motivation, or whether talent will necessarily turn into wealth generation. It is also unnecessary to do so; it will show up in results.

Talent rarely has the right price. At the very beginning of its career, talent is overpaid. Before long, if talent mutates into wealth-creating ability, it is underpaid.

The price of wealth creators is a function of reputation and self-confidence. The two go together, but are far from perfectly correlated. To observe this, go into any bar just before it closes. Reputation is rarely equal to wealth-creating capacity. In the early years of a truly exceptional wealth creator, wealth ability exceeds reputation. In the later years, with few exceptions, it is the other way round. The exceptions are rarely available as employees. When they are, they are the best value of all.

3 Appreciate the value of young talent

80/20 people snap up the particular brand of young talent with wealth-creation potential, before that potential is appreciated. At first, the deal favors talent. Then the talented are converted, as quickly as possible, into wealth creators. At this stage, the 80/20 employer has a great bargain. The 80/20 employer knows that wealth creators must, by definition, be many times—on average 16 times—more effective than the merely competent majority. Therefore, 80/20 employers take great pains to coach and develop talented young people, until the latter have absorbed the powerful business genes and are living exemplars of the 80/20 principle. If some of the talented people do not turn into wealth creators, the 80/20 employer has made a hiring error and must correct it.

The value of young talent is still greater than its price, although the gap for some types of talent is closing. For example, new business graduates (MBAs) from Massachusetts Institute of Technology were paid 60 percent more in 1998 than in 1994, while the earnings of 45–54-year-old male college graduates over the past quarter century actually fell (in inflation-adjusted dollars) by 24 percent.[9] The young are getting more expensive, the old cheaper. Still, in value terms, the young are often cheap and the old are often dear. The young have a greater capacity to import the most powerful business genes and to ferret out new ones.

Older employees may be a self-selected group. More often than not, they have remained employees because they have failed to become wealth generators, or failed to realize that they are, or failed to keep a fair share of the wealth they create. The very many people who fall into the last two categories are extremely important exceptions. Much of this book is written for them. They have learnt to generate wealth but not yet to gain the money and control over their lives that it should bring. They are failing to keep what is rightfully theirs.

When one pool of talent becomes expensive, switch to another pool with many of the same characteristics but much lower demand.

MBA students used to be good value; now they are over-priced. The same goes for Brits: The transatlantic brain-drain has stopped flowing, for good reasons. Freshly minted college graduates used to be fantastic value; now they are merely cheap. My advice is to go hire those who are under-qualified but extremely bright and cheap: graduates in unfashionable subjects (the humanities), drop-outs, 18-year-olds who perform very well on objective tests, or people from "cheap" countries that have good educational systems (try India, South Africa, or New Zealand).

Avoid talent pools that your competitors frequent. Your competitors here are any firms with business genes—the ability to convert talent to wealth—that are as good as or better than yours.

Track the conversion rate from talent to wealth creator for each talent pool. Compare the rate and the value to the cost. Divert your recruitment accordingly.

You should always pay wealth generators more than they expect and less than they are worth. This leaves a wide margin for arbitrage, for appropriating a fat surplus. Be generous early, before it is too late.

Finally, raise the average money-making capacity, or potential capacity, in the firm with each new hire. Many bosses tend to hire those with whom they are most comfortable, who won't challenge their superiority. This is a big mistake. For positive arbitrage, hire the very best people you can find, especially if they are better than you or might become better than you. Only hire people who have the potential to be your partner. Even if they eventually leave, you'll benefit immensely from them.

In sum:

❖ Hire the type of young talent that can become wealth generators quickly.
❖ Of these, hire the cheapest; the market for young people is highly imperfect.
❖ For any given level of talent and wealth-creation potential, favor the under-confident and beware of the over-confident. The former are likely to stay longer after they have become powerful wealth generators.
❖ Overpay young wealth creators, those whom you or others have successfully taught the wealth-creation apprenticeship. Qualified apprentices are always terrific value, even when they are overpaid. Lock them in.
❖ Help talented people who fail to become wealth generators find a great job in another firm, where they can be nicely overpaid by somebody else.
❖ Be careful to spot, hire, and nurture older employees who are genuine wealth creators, and who do not realize or capitalize on their value.
❖ Hire to raise the average in the firm, however high it is already. Hire people whose potential ability to create wealth is greater than yours.

How to lock in great people

Being open-handed early on creates maximum personal loyalty. However bountiful you are, if you are dealing with a young wealth creator, you're almost certainly getting a better deal than he or she is.

Bill Bain, when boss of the eponymous management consultancy, made a habit of making his young super-stars "partners" about a year before they could reasonably expect it. He knew another clever trick. He told them that they were going to become partners about six months before the event. So he got the motivational benefit of the appointment some time before he had to pay for it; six months is a long time in consulting. Those of us who were the beneficiaries felt enormously grateful to Bill. The only cost to him was an early decision. The "partners" tended to overlook the fact that they had only tiny shares of the partnership, and that Bill held on to most of the equity.

When you wish to lock in genuine partners rather than employees, it pays to be generous with the equity. Ensure that you give a higher share than the prospective partner expects, and perhaps than he or she deserves. This is particularly true if the partner-designate is younger or less experienced and has not yet reached his potential. Wealth-creating ability is a moving target; a partner's equity share is usually not. Overshoot now and you'll still be in the money.

When Jim Lawrence proposed forming a partnership with Iain Evans, to form what shortly after became The LEK Partnership (when I joined), Jim offered an equal stake to Iain, despite the fact that Iain had reported to Jim and was substantially less senior. At the time that decision seemed fantastically generous; with hindsight it was one of the best decisions Jim ever made.

Money matters a great deal, but friendship and fun also count. Although this is a controversial view, I hold that you should only hire people whom you like and who like you.

Work is often a bitch, but fun is important for economic as well as non-economic reasons. Fun is a good investment. Fun works. It has a high return on capital, even a high return on management effort. Fun is a bargain.

I don't mean that you should take everyone out for slap-up meals (well, not very often!) or engage in frivolity. I do mean that you should build time for recreation, both individual and social, into the work schedule, and that when work stops being fun, you should find out why and do something about it. If you think you can't afford this, you don't have an 80/20 enterprise. If you are making proper use of the 80/20 principle, you should be highly profitable while also paying tip-top rates and having time for fun.

As Rachel told me, "Work can be boring and serious, or it can be fun. When I go to the head office, all that corporate stuff really is so tedious. All those long faces and frowns and formal meetings. When I get back here [to her office], it's different. I can express myself, we can all express ourselves. We do all the fun things together. We like each other. We make sure we have a good time. I don't feel guilty about it or think it's inappropriate. If we didn't get on so well we couldn't keep raising the profits year after year."

The virtuous cycle of having great people

Once you have a core group of great people, you've entered a virtuous cycle. It becomes easier to attract other great wealth creators. Your firm's reputation is enhanced. You have great morale, productivity, and profitability. These attributes, in turn, make it still easier to enlist even stronger wealth creators. These in turn add to profits, which add to the firm's ability to reinvest in what produces the profits... and so on, until you become complacent, arrogant, or unlucky.

If you sense the momentum of the virtuous cycle faltering, the first leading indicator is likely not your sales or profits—it's the departure of some of your great people. One or two is OK, but more than this is not a coincidence. Only immediate extreme measures will stop the virtuous cycle going into reverse.

What to do if great people leave

If one or two leave, hire some more people with great potential. Take great care this time. Aim not just to raise the firm's average, but to hire people with potential to be better than those who have left. Before long, this should raise your profitability.

If more than a few leave, panic. Find out why. Don't accept the polite answer. Probe for the real reasons. Talk to your other best people. Ask for their recommendations. Do everything they say, and more.

The value of oddballs

The theories of natural selection and of business genes tell us that, in business as in life generally, the key ingredient is diversity. Diversity enhances efficiency. Homogeneity leads to death.[10]

Most people do not like too much diversity, especially in their colleagues. They like people who are like them. Take note of popularity, but put colleagues in a position to surprise themselves in their recruitment decisions.

Deliberately seek out recruitment candidates from unusual backgrounds—whatever is unusual for your firm: ethnic minorities, gays, foreigners, poor people, rich people, under-qualified people, over-qualified people, cultured people, street people—and make it a rule that one new hire in three (or two, or four) has to be from an unusual background. Oddballs should still be popular with your team; it just means that you interview more people.

Whether we like it or not—and I personally do—affirmative action works. So does immigration. Without wave upon wave of immigrants, America and Europe would be much less wealthy.

Make your venture a beacon, if not to the huddled masses, then at least to the vital few among them: a refuge for truly talented and motivated people from unconventional backgrounds, people who would not normally get a break in your business. Take Bill Bain as an example. When he was hired by Bruce Henderson in the early days of the Boston Consulting Group, Bill had no business degree, in fact he knew nothing about business.[11] He had been a bible salesman and a college official raising funds from alumni. Yet he went on to become the biggest individual wealth generator in consulting for a generation.

Encourage "immigration" of oddballs to your team. But realize that immigration is never an easy process and needs to be *managed*. Make sure that there is enough affinity between the new oddball and your existing staff for the mix to work. Ensure that the oddball is fully integrated into the firm's normal processes, not left as an island of eccentricity.

The human side: The theory of the tribe

The new field of evolutionary psychology[12] says that business conditions have changed enormously since the Stone Age, but humans have not. None of us is rational about our place of work; a much more accurate view is that we are quivering masses of emotion, looking for a tribe to belong to and our natural place in its pecking order.

We herd. We conform. We want someone else to lead us. We are friendly to those inside the tribe and suspicious of those outside. We avoid risk. We reject criticism of ourselves. We jump to conclusions based on first impressions. Above all, we want to identify with a small tribe, of no more than 150 people, whom we can know by face and name. In the Stone Age these attributes worked: They facilitated survival. Today they are often a trap.

Note that for most people the tribe is not a whole firm, not if it is large. The tribe is generally a department or other sub-unit that has frequent face-to-face interaction and a common purpose. In a new venture the tribe should be, and usually is, the whole firm.

What are the implications for 80/20 people?

❖ Everybody wants a cohesive tribe and you must create one—the people must like each other and work well together. At LEK Consulting we gave due weight in hiring to the social side: Would our people enjoy working with the new recruit?

❖ You will find it easier to winkle people out of their existing corporations if their need for a tribe can be better met in the new venture than in the old one. If they are happy in their current tribe, it will be virtually impossible to dislodge them.

❖ If the people you want in your new venture are already happy together in your existing firm, that is a very strong reason for doing a deal with your corporation for a joint venture or other hybrid solution (see Chapter 8).

❖ The ideal position for a leader wanting to set up a new independent venture is to have the tribe in your existing company begging for you to lead them to the promised land. It worked for Moses and it will work for you—but only if the tribe really feels this way. To found a spin-off, lead from behind.

❖ Once you have your new venture, exploit tribalism. Happy tribes stick together. People on the edge of the tribe are at least a third out of the door already. If you want to keep someone who is not fitting in, take pains to integrate them: Ensure that they have at least a couple of buddies with whom they click.

The primacy and power of partners

Don't imagine that you are immune to the need for a tribe. Leaders in particular get lonely: They are structurally cut off, at least to some degree, from everyone else. If you want to be happy as well as successful, the only answer is to have at least one excellent partner. You need someone who complements your skills, but, more importantly, is a trusted soulmate: somebody with whom you share all your wild dreams, all your doubts and self-doubts, and all the ups-and-downs and twists-and-turns of the rollercoaster that is a new venture.

Don't start an enterprise without at least one partner. I can't think of a successful and happy 80/20 person, among the hundreds I have known, who didn't have at least one close business partner. In contrast, I can think of several control freaks who don't have a partner. Some of them are even successful, but none appears happy or fulfilled.

The ideal number of partners is between two and seven. More than seven and you lose intimacy and are in danger of cliques forming.

Partners really are the most vital, and fewest, of the vital few. And when you are in business with real partners, make the most of it. Do some business meetings and trips together, even if this seems inefficient. Go into each partner's house (or have them in yours) at least once a week. Keep renewing your sense of partnership. Nothing is more precious, nor more essential, for both success and happiness.

Venture DNA

There is much loose talk today about the "DNA" of particular firms. It is a more apt metaphor than most of its users know. Firms are unique not merely because of the mix of people within them, but because of the business genes within them. The business genes often stay longer than the people.

Teams, firms, industries, and markets are living entities that seethe with a constant bubble. The bubble is the interaction between the business genes, between the genes and the people, and between the people themselves. Effective firms, industries, and markets work simply because they gel. The business genes gel with each other and with the people; the people gel with each other and with powerful business genes.

Like natural selection, the process is evolutionary and unpredictable. There must be constant variation, constant improvement, constant rejection of the majority of variants, constant elaboration of the minority of successful variants.

Don't picture yourself in a white coat, masterminding the genetic mix. You and all your people constitute the stuff in the test tube. If you are successful, it is because you are riding great business genes and cooperating usefully with them. If they find a better vehicle, you are finished. If all your great individual wealth creators latch on to the business genes, and think they can do so better outside than inside your venture, you are finished too.

Keeping the right people gelling with the right genes, with each other and you is a tricky business. Humility, shrewdness, creativity, calculation, luck, experimentation, friendliness, realism, the ability to cooperate with the best cooperators—all of these are necessary to keep your team's DNA alive and well.

The stories of Anton and Jamie

There is one further point about enlisting great individuals. There is a chain of personal links between young money makers and their more experienced counterparts that can be hugely valuable. The patron/protégé relationship is important, not only in one firm but over time, in many business relationships. The younger person is taught how to exploit powerful business genes, gains confidence, and rapidly learns how to create value. In the early stages, greater value passes to the protégé; soon, he or she is adding much more value than he or she takes. At some stage, the younger person either becomes a partner in the business, or is likely to depart for a business with a substantial ownership stake. Yet that is not the end of the story.

Anton and Jamie were protégés of mine, initially at LEK Consulting. They have since started their own ventures, Anton in the fulfillment of direct sales orders and Jamie in venture capital (you met Jamie in Chapter 3). We stay in close touch and continue to add great value to each other. We swap investment opportunities, leads on business opportunities, and, most important of all, leads on talented people who can become money makers for us.

As with most 80/20 people, we've started a chain of mutual person-to-person benefit that will probably still be going strong long after the three of us have shuffled off this mortal coil. This is the model for value creation in the future economy: a club of individuals helping each other find and exploit ideas to create wealth, regardless of corporate affiliation.

The story of Rachel

One reason Rachel fascinates me is that she has generated wealth but not yet taken it. She knows she creates wealth, although she is always careful to include her team. Why hasn't she taken the initiative to start her own business, or to redefine the terms of engagement with her corporation?

When I talk to her about this, she is ambivalent. On the one hand, she says, "What I hate is having this very successful business and yet being inside a corporation that is so spectacularly unsuccessful at everything else." On the other hand, she is reluctant to leave the corporate womb.

In 2001 she became part of a management buyout team. The initiative for the MBO came from her boss and from a private equity firm.

However, as the manager in charge of the most valuable part of the company, she stood to make maybe $10 million or so after three years if the MBO proceeded according to plan. In exchange, she had to make an investment of $60,000 in the deal and undertake some legal "warranties."

Rachel went along with the MBO, but hated the uncertainties and the twists and turns of the buyout process itself. At the last minute the deal was pulled, for reasons unrelated to Rachel or her business. Was she disappointed? "A bit," she answers, "but relieved is nearer the mark. I don't want to go through that process again.

"Management buyouts," she continues, "are all very well if all you're interested in is money. Well, I'm not. I like money, but I have enough of it already. What is important to me is the quality of my life—my working life and my non-working life. My working life depends on the people I work with. I don't want to report to venture capitalists again."

I try again. Everything she says may be true, but is she really happy with the deal she and the team have today? I spell out the wealth they've created. I compare that to their compensation. Aren't they getting short-changed along the way? Never mind the money itself, isn't it unfair?

"My team feels it's unfair. Head office annoys them. When they hired the French chef for lunches, that was the last straw. What annoys my people is how much some of the head office people earn, they think that's unfair. The bonus scheme is OK. They could earn more elsewhere but we like working together. Millions and millions of dollars… it's not something they think they can get. They're not keyed into the financial community. They don't get exposed to those opportunities.

"Look, they were excited by the MBO, and very disappointed when it went away. They were also upset that no one from head office apologized. I was relieved because I felt it was all going to be my responsibility, that all the profits would have to be generated by me. I would feel responsible for Jason's mortgage and Jayne's children's education and all the rest if anything went wrong. The private equity people behind the deal made no attempt to get to know me and reassure me. Faced with a choice between venture capitalists and the status quo, I prefer the latter."

I tell Rachel there is a third option. We're about to explore it.

Notes and references

1 I am grateful to Geoffrey R. Vautier for pointing out the arithmetic behind
   the 80/20 principle. Geoff runs The 80/20 Consulting Company Limited in
   New Zealand. Email: results@the8020co.co.nz.

2 Josef Steindl (1965) *Random Processes and the Growth of Firms: A Study of the
   Pareto Law*, London, Charles Griffin, p. 18.

3 For those who like algebra, here is Pareto's formula. Call N the number of
   income earners who receive incomes higher than x, with A and m being the
   constants. Pareto found that:

$$\text{Log } N = \log A + m \log x$$

   Isn't it interesting that the business gene of algebra is often less powerful than
   that of words, because words are more accessible? If Pareto had expressed his
   insight in the terms it acquired a generation later—the words expressing the
   80/20 principle—he would have had much more influence in his lifetime.

4 Martin Wolf (2001) "Growth makes the poor richer," *Financial Times*, 24
   January, p. 17.

5 Lester C. Thurow (1999) *Creating Wealth: The New Rules for Individuals,
   Companies, and Countries in a Knowledge-Based Economy*, Nicholas Brealey,
   London, Chapter 3.

6 *Ibid.*, Chapter 10. Thurow's source is the Federal Reserve Board, 1995 data.

7 See Richard Koch (1997) *The 80/20 Principle*, Nicholas Brealey,
   London/Currency Doubleday, New York, Chapters 1 and 13.

8 This is a hint to doctoral students at universities and business schools. The
   science of success is a powerful business gene, so please start applying academic rigor to it. It is a great way to make your name. Please send a copy of
   your research to Richardjohnkoch@aol.com.

9 Lester C. Thurow (1999) *Creating Wealth*, Chapter 7.

10 There is a great deal of scientific evidence to support the contention that
   diversity works. See Richard Koch (2001) *The Natural Laws of Business*,
   Currency Doubleday, New York, Chapters 1 and 4. As Charles Darwin
   observed in *The Origin of Species*, "unless profitable variations occur, natural
   selection can do nothing."

11 Except how to sell, a quality that is blithely ignored or under-valued in most
   strategy consultancies.

12 See Chapter 4 of Richard Koch (2001) *The Natural Laws of Business*.

8 *Enlist Your Firm*

"No matter where you work, you are not an employee. You are in business with one employer—yourself ... Nobody owes you a career—you own it as a sole proprietor."

Andy Grove, CEO, Intel Corporation

By now you should know the play and the cast: the new business you will create and who will do it with you. But where? Should you leave your firm, or stay within it?

Can the 80/20 principle help you decide? Yes. The 80/20 principle can guide you to finding a super-profitable business, one where the return on capital is very high. The 80/20 principle also shows us that individuals and their ideas for new businesses are the key thing in creating value.

Therefore, if you have learnt how to create extraordinary value—perhaps after trying a dummy run at it in your existing firm—you would be short-changing yourself to remain within your existing firm. If you use the 80/20 principle for your firm, the firm is almost certainly exploiting you.

An 80/20 person inside someone else's corporation will typically produce returns for the corporation that are between 20 and 200 times his or her compensation.[1] You can load yourself up with stock options and bonuses, but there is no way that most ordinary corporations can pay 80/20 people what they are worth. And the better you are at creating wealth using the 80/20 principle, the more acute this problem will become.

So to get reasonable value—to enjoy a relationship between value creation and value capture that is not insulting—you cannot stay within your firm. It is a short hop to concluding that you should therefore leave the firm and start your own business. The trouble with this conclusion is that it is a purely economic one. Decisions on whether to stay or go are not, and should not be, purely economic. Social and personal considerations also apply. Maybe you like where you work and the people with whom you work. Maybe they couldn't or wouldn't join you in the new venture. Maybe you don't like the risk and hassle involved in going it alone.

Happily, you may be able to have your monetary cake and still enjoy the social experience of eating it. The choice is not exclusively between the alternatives of staying or leaving. In defiance of both traditional physics and management theory, you may be able to do both at the same time.

Rocking Frog: The third way

Jerry Bowskill, who as I write is launching a new venture called Rocking Frog, used to work for BT, the UK telecommunications giant. "We had come to the conclusion," he says, "as a group of friends, that our idea had enormous value. We had taken two holidays from BT and written a business proposition with the help of some friends down the pub who were City traders. But we didn't have enough money and were about to remortgage our houses, when Brightstar came along."[2]

Brightstar is the new BT "incubator" set up in a 100-acre site in the wilds of Norfolk, England. The deal is that entrepreneurial BT employees work within Brightstar to hone their ideas alongside third-party venture capitalists, and then go out to found their new ventures. Even when independent, they can tap into BT's ideas and marketing channels. For this, BT takes between 30 and 40 percent of the new venture.

It seems a good deal for both Jerry Bowskill and his mates, and for BT. Rather than go out directly, says Jerry, "We decided that we had a chance to stay in BT. The downside was that we got less of the business, but the upside is that the business will be much bigger, because we are fully supported by BT and can use its channels to market. Without Brightstar we would have left, and BT would have had nothing in return. There have been many, many friends of ours in a similar position who have left BT. It's the same for all technology industries over the last couple of years."

The top accounting firm of PricewaterhouseCoopers has a slightly different incubator deal. It has just spun off one company, Cataloga, and is about to launch four other new ventures. Unlike BT, PwC puts up some seed capital, but it takes a similar stake, about 30 percent. Interestingly, PwC professionals who leave the firm have an escape hatch back in if the venture folds.

Incubators were set up to cash in on the internet bubble and to avoid losing value creators. The second is clearly a more durable reason. In fact, the incubator model is applicable to any business, whether high tech, low tech, or no tech, and was used informally for many years before business incubators started.

The story of Rick

In the movie *The Firm*, William Devasher is the crooked law firm's security chief, played with powerful malevolence by Wilford Brimley. It so happens that my American friend Rick Haller bears an uncanny resemblance to Devasher/Brimley.

I was a BCG consultant when I first met Rick back in 1979. He was heading the merchant banking operation at Libra Bank, a consortium of leading world banks set up to exploit lending to Latin America. Rick was a natural wealth creator: He set up the merchant banking operation in

Libra from scratch, and by 1980 it was making about $25 million in prof-
its, with a return on average capital employed between 50 and 100
percent.

When I first interviewed him, Rick was open about his belief that his
deal with Libra was unsatisfactory: "Here I am making all this money for
them, and I just draw a decent salary. This is not fair compensation, but
with our shareholders and all their red tape it would take years to sort it
out."

Rick's opportunity to leave, with some 20 of the top fellow wealth
creators in his team, came in 1980 when the shareholders decided to dis-
member Libra in any case. Rather to my surprise, Rick asked my advice
in setting up his new venture.

His problem was that his group needed some lines of capital to support its debt-trading operation, far more than he and his friends could
stump up. He also needed the respectability of an established banking
base, so that other banks would be willing to accept him as a counter-
party. But he was clear about what he wanted: total autonomy for his
group, and a significant share of the profits.

He got it. He constructed a deal with the old-established City of
London investment bank Morgan Grenfell (later Deutsche Morgan
Grenfell, now Deutsche Bank). The Emerging Markets division of DMG
was set up as a "bank within a bank" and Rick's group shared 23 percent
of the annual profits while providing none of the capital. I estimate that
his group made hundreds of millions of dollars profit between 1980 and
1998, when Rick left the bank.

The story of Richard

This is not me, but a successful investment banker based in London.
Richard worked for one investment bank, then moved to another, then
joined another as managing director. Since his love was doing corporate
finance deals, he hated the administrative duties that came with being the
boss. He therefore moved on to another bank and this was where, around

1990, I first had a serious conversation with him about starting his own business. It went something like this:

Me: "You're creating a lot of value. Why not set up your own boutique and keep all the profits?"

Him: "You're right. I'll think about it."

In the end he decided not to. "I'm not sure the time is right. If I can pull off a couple of the huge deals I'm working on, then the timing would be better. Besides, I have my doubts about corporate finance boutiques. At the end of the day, clients like advice, but they like money better. They want to be able to finance deals, to have underwriting. Banks with capital can do that at a stroke. A boutique has to go looking."

However, before long Richard moved again, this time back to the second bank he had worked for. "But this time the deal is different," he told me. "I get to keep a high proportion of the profits I generate."

The story of Richard shows that money makers can enlist employers and strike their own deals. You don't need to have a team, as my friend Rick did. You can do it as an individual, provided that you can generate profits yourself. In investment banking and corporate finance this is most transparent. The fun will come when the same principle is extended to other businesses.

Are consulting firms models for the future?

The consulting industry, where I deposited my youth, provides a variety of reward models. They are interesting because the issues faced by consulting firms and their owners may be a taste of what is to come in business generally. Consultants are classic "knowledge workers" who are, in theory at least, mobile. It is easy for consultants to take the intellectual property of their previous firm; in fact, it is unavoidable. So whatever industry you are in, if you want to be part of a new venture, there may be something to be learnt from consultants about the nature of equity and the rewards necessary to motivate both entrepreneurs and employees.

How to expropriate the owners

When Bruce Henderson set up The Boston Consulting Group in 1963, he did a deal with the Boston Safe and Deposit Company, which provided the modest working capital needed to launch BCG. In the early 1970s, when BCG was already a raging success, it became clear that there was a conflict between the value creators within the business and the bank that owned it. The solution was for BCG professionals to buy the company with its own cash flow, setting up an Employee Stock Option Plan (ESOP) in which all professional staff participated.

In effect, BCG is now run as a professional partnership, sharing the profits among its staff, but retaining a significant portion of each year's profits and only paying them out over time as they "vest" for individuals. That way, BCG has working capital for expansion (and to cushion the occasional poor year) and is able to use the earned but not vested portion of pay to encourage its best professionals to stay. The senior vice-presidents at BCG make high six-figure sums in an average year, and low seven-figure sums in great years, but are not able to make the instant millions that would come from selling the firm.

Who should own knowledge firms like consultancies?

When a professional firm is sold, some partners can make tens of millions of dollars in one fell swoop. For example, Goldman Sachs floated in 1999 and as I write is worth $43 billion. More than 60 percent of that belongs to insiders.

What is interesting is that Bruce Henderson, the founder of The Boston Consulting Group, chose to take only very modest returns from BCG. He was a passionate believer in the free market, but not for himself. He had no regrets, taking great pride in its profound influence and international expansion.

"When he set up BCG," senior vice-president Barry Jones tells me, "Bruce did an extraordinary thing. Rather than keep the equity for himself he gave it to the employees. He created BCG as an inverted pyramid, as a flat structure. As a partner of 18 years, my share of the equity is only twice that of a new partner."

In splitting off from BCG in 1970, Bill Bain pursued a different model. Right until his withdrawal from the business in 1990, he retained ownership of a majority of Bain & Co.'s equity. At the top of the market the firm was sold to its professional staff, who funded the deal with a boat-load of debt, just in time for a market downturn. Despite its terrific business formula and wonderful work, Bain's future hung in the balance for several months. It is now effectively a partnership like BCG and McKinsey.

McKinsey is a most interesting case. Insiders claim that were it not for the lingering influence of Marvin Bower, McKinsey's leader between 1937 and 1960, the firm would have gone public in the 1990s, as younger partners lobbied for a deal that would make their fortunes. Bower's stern rectitude blocked a deal. After all, in 1963, when he reached 60, Bower had sold his shares back to the Firm at book value, a tradition that retiring partners have had to follow ever since.

In 1983, LEK broke away from Bain & Co. My partners and I were sued by Bain, perhaps to discourage other partners from leaving. I am very grateful to Bain for this: It made us feel that the equity in LEK was valuable (we had done nothing wrong and after a few months we reached agreement with Bain's lawyers). When I "retired" from LEK after six years and sold my shares back to the other partners, I was able to argue that the equity should be valued on a market-related basis. Over a decade later, however, there is no sign that LEK is going to float.

At the height of the dot-com mania, many industry insiders thought that the pressure to float the "e-business" parts of firms like McKinsey and The Boston Consulting Group would be irresistible, and that consequently the whole practice would need to be floated, to prevent internal defections to the e-business. The collapse in internet stock market valuations came just in time to prevent this.

When a professional firm floats or sells itself, its current partners are really cashing in on both the past and the future. They are coining in the goodwill and reputation of the firm's brand, built up over many generations of partners, and they must also necessarily be short-changing the

future professionals. A consulting partnership is as near to a perfect mer-
itocracy as is possible in this life (which in my experience is not that perfect, but let that pass).

If one particular firm, McKinsey for illustration, does not go public,
then future McKinsey partners will share the total future annual profits
of the Firm. If the Firm does go public, it will have to declare earnings
and dividends for its public owners, and therefore the partners will get
less. They will get a nice income, but they will not enjoy the profits on
top. It follows that for all professionals, advancement to the partnership
would not be as attractive as it used to be.

That is why when the partners of professional firms sell out, those in
the next level down, the so-called "mezzanine layer," are often hopping
mad. Many defect to other firms and a few set up on their own. This
result has prompted some firms that float to do something for the mezzanine layer, yet what can be done may not be enough, and there is always
a knock-on effect further down the professional chain. For ordinary consultants, to have your partners sell out is bad news.

In professional firms that don't float or sell themselves, the senior professionals progressively share in something that is more than they themselves create. The top people in The Boston Consulting Group make not
only what they could make outside, which is their sustainable income,
but also the profits of the firm as well.

The profits derive, of course, from each year's work, yet they are not
the result of the aggregate professional skill of the firm's members. The
profits also derive from the firm's reputation and brand, which in older
consulting firms will have been largely established before the current
generation of partners took over. My friends at the top of BCG are
benefiting from what Bruce Henderson created.

My McKinsey mates are drawing on the "rent" that Marvin Bower
put into the McKinsey name. The BCG and McKinsey partners cannot
make a large one-off fortune by selling out, but they are content to stay
and make small fortunes each year.

When I talk to people at all levels in consulting firms, it becomes clear
that the partnership model is both sustainable and attractive.

The story of Barry

Barry Jones, a senior vice-president at The Boston Consulting Group and a former close colleague of mine there, makes a telling point. "We are building a virtuous circle here," he comments. "I've been here for 25 years, and if you had told me that I would be with one firm for that long when I joined I'd have said you were nuts. But, after 25 years, amazingly, I am still very happy here. It really feels like a family, it's a collegiate, fantastic organization.

"Yes, I do feel fairly rewarded. I could probably get more money outside, doing some job that I didn't really like, but money is not the be-all and end-all of life. For me, the combined financial and lifestyle package presented by BCG as a partnership is far more sustainable than that of a company on the stock exchange, or of the deal-based culture of an investment bank. In neither would I feel that I am my own boss in the same way as at BCG.

"Over time, the firm and its brand become worth more and more. This gives a comfortable income to the vice-presidents, and also acts as a magnet for our professional staff—not just the ones we have now, but also the ones we want in the future. By the time they become officers of the firm [partners], they and the current generation of officers will have made it even more valuable.

"Other human benefits," Barry goes on, "are important too. Socially, many of my friends are inside the firm, or were at one time. My colleagues' wives are friends with mine. Professionally, I enjoy the opportunity to spend time on things like developing the firm's intellectual capital—I'm currently head of its strategy practice. These are investments in the firm's library. You can't afford them if you are too interested in this year's profits and share price. At times, work in BCG is hard and the hours can be long, but I wouldn't say it's stressful. The partnership ethos is very real and colleagues support each other."

I asked Barry if BCG would ever sell out. "Emphatically, no. Because of the environment, we did look at it in the past two years but quickly dismissed it. If we sold the company we'd be betraying what we believe

in and what makes BCG what it is. If someone wanted to propose that
we sell, the rules are one partner, one vote, and a high acceptance hurdle.
The younger partners want to work here for a lifetime—why would they
sell out? And the older partners realize that what we enjoy today is purely
a function of what was created in the past. More than 80 percent of us
feel a real moral obligation to maintain the institution rather than make
a quick buck that we don't need anyway."

The story of Donna and Jeff

The power of professionals within consulting or investment banking
firms is matched by what managers in conventional firms can do, so long
as they know the value they provide. This is demonstrated by the story of
Jeff Hawkins and Donna Dubinsky, the inventors of the PalmPilot electronic personal organizer.

Jeff and Donna would have liked to raise money from venture capitalists, but the latter "knew" that handheld organizers were a sure-fire
route to the poor house. So Jeff and Donna settled in 1995 for $44 mil-
lion from a corporation, U.S. Robotics.

Initially it worked out fine. U.S. Robotics "let us run Palm indepen-
dently ... They were more like our bank than our boss," Donna said
later.[3] To the astonishment of the venture capitalists, PalmPilots went bal-
listic. But then the downside of taking the corporate coin emerged.

In 1996, U.S. Robotics was taken over by 3Com. 3Com tried to run
PalmPilot as an integrated division. Jeff and Donna lost autonomy. They
also lost money, as 3Com stock (the consideration they ended up with
for selling PalmPilot) tanked.

Thus began a war of nerves between Jeff and Donna, and Eric
Benhamou, the 3Com CEO. Spin PalmPilot off, begged Jeff and Donna.
No way, replied Eric. (By 1998, PalmPilot was the only bright spot in
3Com's world.) But Eric knew that Jeff and Donna held the better cards.
They could always set up a competitor to PalmPilot.

Jeff and Donna did set up a new venture, Handspring, in 1999. Eric agreed to license the Palm operating system to them. He really had no choice. As Donna put it, "The alternative [for 3Com] was to push us into the arms of Palm operating system competitors or recreate a similar operating system ourselves. They knew it would be smarter to have us as their platform product partner."

What Donna tactfully does not say is that Handspring's purpose was to create a cheaper and better alternative to the Palm line. As I write, it is executing this with great panache.

What do we make of the story of Jeff and Donna?

❖ It is always a mistake to imprison 80/20 people in a corporate structure they cannot control and in which they do not have an ownership stake that is directly related to their venture. This was bad for all concerned: for Jeff and Donna, and for 3Com shareholders.

❖ Whatever the previous deal and whatever the ownership structure, the value creators like Jeff and Donna hold the whip hand. Value will out. Any value creator who is determined to capture the value that he or she creates can do so. A big corporation can buy an enterprise, products, and patents, but if the key people leave, so too does the growth.

❖ A "hybrid" deal between value creators and their corporation—like the one that Jeff and Donna eventually ended up with—is often best for everyone. But the value creators must have autonomy and an equity stake in their own venture.

What do Jerry, Rick, Richard, Bruce, Barry, Jeff, and Donna mean for you?

Alongside the two traditional routes for entrepreneurs—the management buyout and buyin, and starting an entirely independent new venture—we can see at least three hybrid structures that are available, and may well be more attractive for some would-be entrepreneurs. The hybrids are basically individual-centered structures—they are run by 80/20 people—but they combine aspects of earlier corporate structures:

❖ The partnership structure (the Barry Jones/BCG solution), where the partners buy the business from its owners and where there is no external equity. The partnership structure is an ancient corporate form yet is well adapted to many fast-growth knowledge businesses, where the need for capital is low and the need to keep and attract money makers is high.

❖ The host/profit-sharing solution, where a new firm is set up within another firm (the Rick Haller/DMG solution). The team has a contractual right to a share of the profits; the host company provides the capital and takes a share of annual profits as well. A similar solution can be applied to individual money makers, as with Richard, my investment banker friend. Another variant is a formal joint venture between a new team of entrepreneurs and an established corporation (which may be the one you work for now, or a third party).

❖ The incubator solution (which also used to be called corporate venturing), where entrepreneurs from one firm found a new venture and the old firm takes a stake (the Jerry Bowskill/Rocking Frog/BT solution). Whether or not there is an incubator, this model is capable of widespread expansion. The bridge between the old firm and the new is seamless and links between them remain in place.

How to enlist your firm

Ask yourself three questions:

❖ Which solutions are potentially available to me? Do they make sense for the other parties involved (my partners, the managers and owners of the firm, providers of capital)?

❖ Out of the viable options, which structure will enable me to create something of greatest value?

❖ Which solution will make me happiest and more fulfilled?

1 Starting a new venture

Clearly, you could start a new venture. The downside is that you have to
leave your current business home, and brands, behind; you may also have
to leave your customers, technology, and key colleagues. If you use capital from other people, especially if it comes from a venture capital institution, your new masters may be more demanding than the old ones. The
upside is that the new business is yours. As long as you meet financial
expectations, you can run it how you want. You will also keep much or
most of the value you create.

The management buyout or buyin option depends on whether you
have a willing seller, on the one hand, and whether you can make a good
return for yourself and the capital provider on the other. The ideal pro-
file for such a business is as follows:

❖ A low market value of the business, as reflected in a low price/earn-
   ings multiple (the total stock market value of the firm divided by its
   earnings). Very often public markets do not like small businesses in
   low-growth markets.
❖ High cash-generation potential. Cash flow is important so that the
   business can be leveraged using debt. A high proportion of debt means
   that less equity from venture capitalists is needed, which means that
   there is more chance of meeting their high rate-of-return requirements—and still leaving money for you in the deal. A high interest
   charge also means that you will pay less tax.
❖ The potential to increase earnings and hence the value of the company when it is sold again.

Management buyouts, especially of large quoted corporations, are a
paradox. Private equity firms who initiate and finance the deals require
a much higher rate of return than do shareholders on the stock
exchange. How, then, can the former outbid the latter to buy the
companies?

The answer lies in three aspects of buyouts:

❖ They rely on under-valuation of the companies. The private equity people have to buy cheap. To some extent, buyouts are a conspiracy between the management and the private equity financiers to pay less to the vendors than the business is really worth.

❖ The buyout vehicle has superior leverage. Public companies do not like to load themselves up with debt. Shareholders don't like debt because it could interfere with the predictability of dividends. Managers don't like debt because it leads to sleepless nights. In the buyout there is usually as much or more debt than there is equity. The equity is more expensive than public money equity, but the debt is much cheaper. The weighted average cost of capital can be lower in a buyout than on the stock exchange. (The risk, of course, is greater.) High leverage brings another benefit: a low rate of taxation. In the early years of a buyout, much of the operating profit goes to pay interest, resulting in a low tax charge.

❖ There is great motivation. In a buyout everyone is focused on achieving financial results, and if they don't come, the consequences are dire for all. In a typical corporation, especially if there are several businesses within it, the managers running any particular division are insulated from financial risk and cannot make their own decisions in response to market developments.

Buyouts are inherently stressful. Yet if the conditions are right, they are a great way to get rich.

The story of Paul

One man who didn't have to worry about dealing with private equity financiers is Sir Paul Judge. Paul was a friend from The Wharton School who seemed to be following a conventional career as a strategic planner at Cadbury Schweppes. In 1986 Cadbury decided to sell its Foods division, which included Typhoo tea and Hartley jams. Paul persuaded Dominic Cadbury, the CEO, to allow him to bid for the Foods division, together with its management. The bid was unusual in that Paul and the other directors managed to fund the deal without any venture capital or private equity money (see Chapter 10).

Paul's bid won. Then came three years in which the magic of the MBO worked wonders in the renamed Premier Brands. Costs previously judged essential by the Foods division management suddenly became surplus to requirements. New products were launched. Market share was gained. Net margins went from 2.1 percent in 1985 to over 8 percent. Profits were £6.6 million in 1985, but £31 million in 1988. Paul and his friends bought the business for £97 million, yet sold it to Hillsdown Holdings, a large corporate, for £310 million in 1989.

Who created this value? Paul and his friends. Who benefited? Paul, his friends, and Cambridge University. Paul alone made over £40 million. Subsequently he gave away a chunk of this wealth to endow the business school at Cambridge University—now called the Judge Institute—with a terrific new building.

I would never discourage a gung-ho entrepreneur like Sir Paul from pursuing a buyout or from setting up his or her own new venture. These moves are good for business and society because they stimulate experimentation, they reduce the degree of "averaging" in the economy, they raise its growth rate, and they help to close the gap between the people who create wealth and where the wealth normally goes. I know many individuals whose lives have been transformed both when buyouts succeed and when they fail. The great thing is that the odds are not symmetrical.

If the buyout or new venture succeeds, nearly everyone's life is improved. The money gained may not in itself make you happy, but financial independence vastly expands the choice you have and frees you up to seek fulfillment in any direction. But even if the business fails, you may still benefit. You will have learnt a lot and you can always have another go—at another new venture or buyout, at the sort of job you did before, or at another career. You may be poorer than before financially, but you will be richer in experience, and you will know the value of experimentation. Many people I know failed in their first new venture or buyout but went on to great things thereafter.

Yet, as with Rachel, *many 80/20 people simply do not want the hassle, risk, legal obligations, and loss of tribal support* that flow from going out on their own.

One solution is to scale down your capital needs, use your savings, and seek backing from family, friends, and business angels. The pressures of starting a new venture will be reduced.

However, there is another option, one not generally considered but that may be much better for 80/20 individuals and for society: to do a deal with your existing company or another company. The hybrid solutions—such as Jerry Bowskill's incubator deal, or Rick Haller's team profit sharing, or Barry Jones' partnership—can work extremely well, and yet involve much less hassle, risk, obligation, and loss of tribal support.

2 Finding a hybrid solution

Hybrid solutions are good for individuals, because they take you at least three-quarters of the way, maybe all the way, to the benefits of having your own business, but at half or less the normal psychic and financial cost. A profit-sharing deal will probably not require you to set up a separate new legal entity. A partnership or incubator deal will not involve the wrench of leaving paid employment to set up a venture, nor of leaving behind your friends and business contacts. In all cases, a new venture can emerge seamlessly from the chrysalis of the old, and the degree of financial risk is reduced, because the corporate partner underwrites some or all of this, either directly or by providing a semi-captive source of finance.

Hybrid solutions are good for established corporations, if new value is created to which they would not previously have had access, and if they can get a share of that new value.

Hybrid solutions are particularly good for the economy and society. This is because they enable more new ventures to be created than would otherwise happen. Good ideas are liberated from companies that might not ever have seen the light of day. Returns are "de-averaged," as those who create wealth take a larger share of it. Individuals have greater control over their working lives and, at the same time or later, over their whole lives. This in turn encourages more individuals to become 80/20 people.

The world of the 80/20 individual is much wider, and less daunting, than the traditional image of entrepreneurs implies. Many 80/20 people have done deals with their corporations and remained part of a tribe throughout. Many more would be willing to have a go, if they knew that such options existed. Now they do.

A word of caution, nevertheless. A hybrid, 80/20 deal with an existing corporation is not to be confused with many initiatives that do come from top management. Profit centers, the creation of "entrepreneurial units" within corporations, the "individualized corporation,"[4] "intrapreneur" programs, and "empowerment" of individuals and teams—these are all attempts to rejuvenate and energize existing corporations, not to encourage new ventures. Such initiatives are welcome; they are likely to do more good than harm. They could easily spill over into hybrid solutions that do involve the creation of new businesses. But unless and until they do, there is no fundamental break with the old way of doing things. The corporation, not the individual, remains the key unit of value creation and value capture.

Three differences separate 80/20 deals from corporate makeovers. A genuine new venture:

❖ Is proposed by an individual or small team and not by the corporate hierarchy.
❖ Involves the transfer of real ownership, or a defined and substantial slice of the profits, to 80/20 people.
❖ Leaves the new team free to run the business how they want, subject only to proper behavior in respect of property (brands, patents, or other shared property) that is still owned by the larger corporation.

More succinctly, it is run by the 80/20 people, for the 80/20 people, with the 80/20 people.

Where much or all of the value in a business transparently belongs to its individual practitioners, such as in Barry Jones' consulting or in Rick Haller's investment banking, then the team creating the value is in a strong position to negotiate with either its current owners or with a new corporate partner. The Boston Consulting Group buys itself out from the Boston Safe and Deposit Company and becomes a partnership. Rick Haller's team goes from one bank to another and writes its own terms.

In most branches of commerce, however, the relative contributions of the individual and small team on the one hand, and the total corporation on the other, are not so clear cut. In practice, they are not worth arguing about. I am not advocating a form of small team trade unionism, where the team creating growth haggles with its employers to gain a share of the profits or to earn equity. It is up to the owners of the corporation and its board to propose whatever compensation they consider in the owners' interests, and if this is not sufficient to clear the market—if the top value creators leave—this is just a miscalculation by the board.

80/20 people take control of their own fate. If an individual's or small team's skills and ability to create wealth are demonstrably portable—as with Rick Haller and his team—they can go and negotiate an entrepreneurial deal with a third-party corporation. As Rick's deal with Morgan Grenfell illustrates, this is possible even when the corporate partner is necessary to complete the ingredients the team needs; in Rick's case, capital and banking status. A deal could be constructed that created wealth both for the 80/20 people and the third-party corporation and if Morgan Grenfell had not agreed, Rick could have gone over the street to another City bank. Richard, the investment banker, did and, even as a one-person business, managed to keep most of his profits.

If the individual and small team want to start a business, but there are doubts about the portability of their skills, it can still be possible for them to create a new venture. They can do so, as we've seen earlier, by appropriating powerful business genes, ideas that enable wealth to be created. Many or most of these ideas may appear to come from the corporation in which the team currently works, but they probably do not belong to the corporation itself. The ideas belong to the industry; in practice, to no one at all.

In trying to prevent my partners and I from setting up in competition with Bain & Co., the latter argued that we had taken its intellectual property. As we successfully pointed out, Bain's intellectual property derived from the industry at large and The Boston Consulting Group in particular. The ideas we took belonged to nobody.

The stories of Gordon, Mark, and Richard

Many entrepreneurs start by evolving a business formula as employees within one firm and then starting their own with a new twist on the same theme. Here are two cases I know.

Professor Gordon Edge was the founder of PA Technology, a division of the management consultancy PA. Although he was the founder, however, Gordon had no equity rights. In the 1980s, PA Technology was very profitable but PA was not. Gordon was a senior director of PA, but poorly compensated. He nearly became PA's chief executive. In the end, someone else was chosen. For Gordon, it was a lucky escape.

In 1986, he set up The Generics Group, commonly known as Generics. "The main difference between Generics and PA Technology," Gordon tells me, "and the reason I left to set up Generics, was that I wanted to actively encourage spinouts and investment in intellectual property rights. Today, Generics is a quoted company on the main London Stock Exchange, with a market value around £100 million. We have 50 companies in our portfolio, of which 15 are spinouts. We also have 15 licenses in place." A number of large corporations, including Siemens in Munich, now use the Generics spinout model.

"We could never have done what we have with Generics, without our earlier experience," Gordon says. "Still, for me the vital thing was to experiment with a more entrepreneurial model. You learn from the past and build on it but then create something new and exciting."

The other example is Richard Burton and Mark Allin, friends working in separate publishing firms who came together to found Capstone Publishing in 1996. "The vision we had for Capstone was really a combination of our experience in working in the other firms, plus our own ideas for creating populist series of books in business publishing," Mark tells me.

"We could never have started so effectively," Richard chips in, "without trial runs in our old firms. We knew what we wanted to do. It didn't seem strange at all doing it for ourselves rather than as a profit center in a much larger firm. The ideas were the important thing."

The story of Rachel

In Rachel's case it is basically the same picture: The powerful business genes that make her current business successful do not belong to her corporation. The idea of design-led segmentation of the market, the idea of concession retailing in department stores, the idea of designing product cost down to take account of the real mix of price realization (that only 40 percent of clothes will be sold at full price), the organization of the business system to minimize the use of capital—these general ideas are powerful business genes and anyone can exploit them.

Yet 80/20 people who have experienced the power of the ideas, and made them work, have huge personal advantages. Rachel and her team are experienced and adept at making the ideas work. They know the specific people to go to outside the corporation in order to create wealth—the individual fabric designers, for example—and how to interact with them.

The parent corporation that owns Rachel's business sits uneasily in the middle of this wealth-creation system. It owns the current business but owns neither the ideas nor the people who make the business possible. Increasingly, all business has these characteristics: increasing the bargaining power of individual and small teams, and eating into that of large firms.

I joke with Rachel that she is only 80 percent of an 80/20 person: "You're missing the vital 20 percent, the ownership that goes with adding value."

Nevertheless, the business does not belong to Rachel's team. She has three choices. She can continue to be an employee, creating wealth and hoping that the corporation notices it and understands that she has transferable skills. She can go the traditional entrepreneurial routes that rely on venture capital: arrange a buyout of her division, for example, or start a new venture from scratch. Or she can pursue the hybrid route, trying to find an alliance with her existing corporation or a new one.

"In theory, the hybrid route you describe appeals to me," she admits, "but what would it mean in practice? Who do I do a deal with?"

"One way," I say, "would be to do a deal with the board [of her current corporation]. Now, the board is there to look after shareholders' interests. The board is not going to let you walk off with the existing business—unless you buy it, and I hear what you say about private equity firms. So, a deal that is in your interests and also in your current firm's interests would have to be a new business. You would have to create something that is separate from the business you now run. In fact, you'd have to find other people to plug the holes left by you and the team members who depart with you. The existing business would have to continue to make profits for its owners. What you would propose, on top of this, would be a share in the new profits that you would create, in a different business."

"But that's difficult," Rachel interposes. "We've already shot ourselves in the foot, in that case, by announcing all our expansion plans—our new brand and a chain of new retail stores. All those ideas now belong to the existing business."

"You're probably right," I concede. "I'm not absolutely sure. For example, I think you could start a new catalog business—selling by mail order and the internet—bolted alongside the existing one. The new business would use some of the property of the existing one like the customer names and addresses, but it could be largely separate. Or maybe you could take the business genes that work so well in the existing market and apply them to a new market—to menswear, for example, or to a non-clothing business, or to a different geography. Any new business that is incremental to the firm's existing profits creates a potential win/win—a win for you and the team, and a win for the board and the current company. You would share in profits that would not otherwise be created.

"My view is that if you really put your mind to it, you could create much more. The world would end up with two businesses, and you would have a substantial stake in the new one. You would need to find some new people to run the new business—some mix of your existing team and the new one—but that could be done. You would be leveraging the business genes that you know work, and your entrepreneurial skill.

"If you can't think of a viable new venture to put alongside the existing business, you still have one other option. You and some of your team can propose a deal to a third-party corporation, to set up a new business—like the existing one but not competing with it too directly, and with a new genetic ingredient, perhaps one derived directly from the third party.

"If you think a menswear business is viable, for instance, it may be sensible to do it in alliance with a company that already has the right customer base or channels to market. If you like the catalog mail-order idea, then it might make sense to team up with a firm that has this expertise already but in other product areas. Of course, these skills might be available from other individuals more cheaply than from corporations. Or you might see real benefits from a joint venture both with your existing firm and a new one, where your team would have a stake and so would each of them."

Individuals can use the 80/20 principle to exploit their corporations...

Individuals and small teams are well positioned to use the 80/20 principle to exploit their corporations, all in a perfectly ethical way. The individuals can identify the few really powerful business genes that may account for most, all, or more than all of the firm's success. Small teams can form, comprising the best users of these business genes, the individuals who are best at using the ideas that power profits. 80/20 people find new ways to exploit the ideas that have made their firm successful, adding new twists to originate distinctive and even more attractive ventures.

...and then choose the ownership solution that suits the individuals best

80/20 people can then either go down the traditional roads to forming a new venture, or can cut their existing firm in on the deal. A hybrid solution—a new business that is a joint venture between the existing firm and 80/20 people—can add profits to the old firm while also getting you started on the road to riches in a way that can be seamless, fast, emotionally satisfying, and less risky than going it alone entirely. Who knows, you may also end up with a bigger business and a bigger fortune to boot!

Notes and references

1   Assume that the 80/20 person creates a new business after five years with profits of $20 million a year and generates net cash over this period. Value the business on a pretax multiple of 10 and it is worth $200 million. Assume that the 80/20 person is paid $200,000 per annum or $1 million over five years. The value created is therefore 200 times the value captured by the individual.

You can play around with the numbers in different ways. Assume that the individual is very highly valued by the company and that it pays him $1 million a year. That still means that he creates 40 times more value than he receives. Or assume that it is really a team of five equal executives, all paid $200,000 a year, who create the business—each one of them still creates 40 times more value than they receive. Whichever way you cut it, 80/20 people who remain employees are underpaid by a huge margin.

2   Quoted in *People Management*, 19 April 2001, p. 34.

3   Aryln Tobias Gajilan (1999) "The parents of the Pilot try for an encore with Handspring: A talk with the Palm pioneers," *Fortune*, Small Business edition, November 22 1999, Special Issue/Businessman of the Century, p. 374.

4   See Sumantra Ghoshal and Christopher A. Bartlett (1997) *The Individualized Corporation*, William Heinemann Random House, London. Oddly, there is no definition of the individualized corporation. It is clear, however, that Ghoshal & Bartlett mean a corporation "built on the bedrock of individual initiative at all levels of the company" (Chapter 2). There is no hint that

individuals may share in ownership. The emphasis is far more on the corporation than on the individual. The authors follow the conventional view that it is corporations rather than individuals that create value: "companies serve as society's main engine of discovery and progress by continuously creating new value out of the existing endowment of resources" (Chapter 10).

9 *Enlist Other Firms*

"There breaks out an epidemic that, in all earlier epochs, would have seemed an absurdity—the epidemic of over-production ... there is too much civilization, too much means of subsistence, too much industry, too much commerce."

Karl Marx and Friedrich Engels[1]

"Companies have grown so productive that their markets can no longer absorb the de facto increases in capacity that continual productivity improvement creates."

Larry Shulman of The Boston Consulting Group[2]

The 80/20 person's privilege is to select only the most profitable activities and most profitable parts of markets: the ones where the very highest returns on capital are made, with the minimum of management effort.

Having found these market fragments and a very limited repertoire of activities, the 80/20 person must serve the customers within these parts of the market far better than anyone else, for the limited activities undertaken. Because they are such profitable areas, you should be able to provide a much better product or service than competitors and still make high returns. "Better" means whatever dimensions the customer values

most, whether speed, convenience, features, quality, design, or even, per-
ish the thought, price.

However, what happens if the most profitable activities cannot be marketed and sold on their own? For example, in Zoffany Hotels, we knew
that the most profitable part of our business was bedrooms and that we
lost money on food and beverage activity. Yet our customers want to be
fed and watered as well as billeted. We could not provide only bedrooms.

The answer is to subcontract the undesired activity to someone else.
That is what Zoffany does with its restaurants. That is what you must do
with any but the most profitable activities. For everything but the most
succulent activities, you must exploit other firms. They are the carriers of
water and hewers of stone. Their role is to do all your heavy lifting.

What happens at the level of the individual venture is writ large for
the economy as a whole. The 80/20 principle shows that only a small
minority of activities fall in the super-profitable pool, the place where
80/20 people swim. So who is to run the rest of the economy, the majority of business activity?

Not 80/20 people. No thank you.

The answer is the same corporations that run the economy today.
Most revenues will fall in the existing corporate sector. The only thing is,
most profits won't. Most profits will belong to 80/20 people.

Our mindset must change. We are no longer the under-dogs. We are
the over-dogs.

We are used to thinking of the individual as the little guy, at the mercy
of the big battalions, twisting and turning to find a niche neglected by
the big boys. This imagery used to be right; no more. The niches today
are not consolations, they are first prizes. A better image is Tom and Jerry:
the happy mouse zooming in to the comfy hole that the fat cat cannot
reach. Or the Flintstones being pulled by a docile brontosaurus.

The large corporations are our brontosauruses. How come? Why are
older and larger firms willing to be used by us, so that we can be so much
more profitable than them?

Over-production arrives at last

We're in the right place at the right time. Corporations have been so productive and capital so plentiful that there is now a serious over-supply of capacity, of the ability to make almost every physical good you could imagine. As Larry Shulman, a senior vice-president of The Boston Consulting Group, says, "More than a decade of investments in information technology and capital-goods spending has finally paid off."[3]

Yet this productivity surge is also a trap for mature companies. Continual productivity gains are headaches if they run ahead of the increase in market demand. And they do. In oil, cars, silicon chips, steel, you name it, capacity is at least a third greater than demand. For mature firms cash piles up, but excess capacity creates a buyer's market and the ever-present threat of price deflation.

The cash itself is also a problem. In the old days, firms with too much cash would simply diversify. The 80/20 principle is sufficiently well understood, by investment analysts if not always by CEOs, to block this route. So, Mr. Shulman suggests, companies are using their excess cash to buy other companies in the same line of business, especially abroad. What looks like rational globalization is in fact driven by having too much cash. But that is another story.[4]

80/20 people benefit from over-production

The benefit from over-production goes to new companies, without productive capacity or the need to acquire it—the company that has customers itself, but can subcontract production of everything but the most profitable activities to other firms.

It is a buyer's market not so much for consumers as for the "in-between" firms, those that sell to consumers or to profitable business customers, but who can source the majority of their needs from industrial firms.

People talk about the internet and excess capacity giving power to customers. That is three-quarters right. Individual consumers have benefited from deflation of prices. Yet the failure of consumer brands to crumble into the dust, and the willingness of consumers to support the economy in good times and bad, are testimony to the resilience of consumer goods suppliers. You would think from what many commentators say about increasing consumer power that the profits of branded goods suppliers would have tumbled. They have not; their profits are generally flat or rising.

What consumer goods firms lose to consumers in lower prices, they more than make back from their suppliers, where they screw down the cost of bought-in goods. The really big winners are industrial buyers. In business-to-business transactions, those who have demand are striking terrific bargains with the poor suckers who are stuck with the supply. The firms that are really winning are those in the middle: generally small, high-growth firms who have increasing demand from customers, but who do not have the capacity to make things. This used to be a quandary for 80/20 people; now it is a godsend.

In many industries new capacity may not be required for many decades—or ever. A new enterprise will need working capital, but it should not need to invest in capital goods, in things that make other things. There is already a glorious over-supply of infrastructure, too much frozen capital. There are too many factories, too many machines within them, too many warehouses, too much retail space, even too many laboratories for research and development.

With machines and buildings go people, trained and ready to produce. There are also too many people. They are all at your command. Rather than close facilities and fire people, managers in mature firms welcome incremental orders from anywhere, almost regardless of their profitability. These managers put their corporate capital, their know-how, their employees, and their contacts—assets that probably took years of blood, sweat and hard cash to build—at your disposal for a knock-down price.

Growth has not stopped. The conditions for growth, recessions notwithstanding, have never been better. What has changed is the *nature* of growth. Growth used to require investment in productive capacity. That job has been done. Today, growth requires new ideas, new inspiration, new business models, variants of existing successful models, and new and better services. The essence of growth used to be physical—now it is mental.

For 80/20 people, this is wonderful. It is unprecedented and epoch making. For the first time, new ventures do not need to create their own corporate infrastructure. You don't need your own factories, warehouses, trucks, shops, offices, or laboratories. You may not even need your own brands or access to customers. You can use the property of older and larger firms. You can rent it, or enter a revenue-sharing or royalty arrangement; in all cases you avoid the need for capital.

You may also be able to buy surplus assets or brands—and perhaps even a whole business—at a fraction of the original cost.

Sometimes you can exploit other firms that are in your line of business, even if you are a potential competitor. If a large and successful firm hasn't been able to make a business work, it won't believe that a start-up could.

Plymouth Gin: How to be a cuckoo

Cuckoos cannot be bothered to raise their young. Instead, they deposit cuckoo eggs in the nests of other species of birds. These unsuspecting parents feed and protect the baby cuckoos. The latter reward this generosity by kicking their pretend siblings out of the nests, or by eating them.

Being a cuckoo is nice work if you can get it. 80/20 people can.

The proof lies in Plymouth Gin. This business dates back to 1793, and at times during the first half of the twentieth century was a leading brand in America, Europe, and what remained of the British Empire. Books of cocktail recipes generally specify the use of Plymouth Gin for pink gin and many other cocktails. The company that owned Plymouth Gin enjoyed a monopoly of it: Whereas "London Dry Gin" can be made anywhere in the world, Plymouth Gin can only be made in Plymouth, England.

During the 1980s control of Plymouth Gin fell to Whitbread, then to Allied Lyons, whose drinks portfolio included another premium gin,

Beefeater. Rather than run two competing top brands, Allied decided to sideline Plymouth Gin.

It made a good job of it. By 1996, sales of Plymouth Gin were negligible. But there was still a large working distillery with the capacity to produce huge volumes of gin. Rather than pay to close it down, Allied Domecq (as it had become) sold the company, brand, and distillery to me and my partners at a knock-down price.

Five years later, the gin world was a different place. In the British premium gin market, Plymouth had overtaken Beefeater. This may not unduly have perturbed Allied Domecq. Although the British drink a great deal of gin, the UK market comprises less than 10 percent of the world total. If Plymouth Gin's resurgence could be confined to Britain, it wouldn't greatly matter to Beefeater, Tanqueray, or Bombay Sapphire.

However in 2000, in a bid to internationalize, Plymouth Gin entered a strategic alliance with Vin & Sprit, the Swedish corporation owning Absolut Vodka. We sold 50 percent of Plymouth Gin to Vin & Sprit for a substantial cash sum, also gaining access to Absolut's global distribution network. In 2001, Vin & Sprit entered joint ventures with both Jim Beam and Maxxium, ensuring that Plymouth Gin could be effectively marketed and sold everywhere around the world.

What had happened? My partners and I had started a new venture by buying a 203-year-old brand and a large distillery from a mature industry leader with excess capacity. I have no idea how much had been invested in the brand and the business over two centuries, but it must have been tens of millions, and possibly hundreds of millions, of dollars. Because of perceived excess capacity, a well-run conglomerate giant was willing to unload this business—a liability or a fabulous heritage, depending on your viewpoint—for a tiny sum.

My partners, John Murphy and Charles Rolls, then built up the business in the UK so that it was sufficiently credible to interest another drinks industry leader. By striking a deal with Vin & Sprit we then acquired the muscle to restore Plymouth Gin to its previous role as one of the world's leading premium gins, an enormously valuable position. If this potential is realized, Allied Domecq, the owner of the Beefeater brand and the company that got us started, will surely rue the day that it sold us its apparently defunct brand and distiller.

Nothing that we did could have been done without the two big, established companies who helped us. Yet they were more than willing to do so. Which mature industry giants are going to help you make a killing?

The story of Bill

Back in the 1980s there was an 80/20 person called Bill. He ran a very small company making very small profits. He worked in the computer industry. His problem was that he didn't know which brand of software was going to win. So he divided his team into several different groups, some working on DOS, some on OS/2, others on SCO Unix, yet others on Mac applications, and other teams on his firm's own developments. It seemed scarcely credible that any of the latter would win against older and better-funded rivals.[5]

Then Bill did something extremely clever. He parlayed his small company into an alliance with IBM, when it was at the height of its fortune. The deal was that Bill's company would develop software for the IBM personal computer (PC), yet with no restriction on the use of that software for other computers. The decision to use "open architecture" helped IBM achieve extraordinary growth in its sales of PCs. It was not, however, profitable growth. The attractive activity—the one that generated a tiny proportion of industry sales, but a high proportion of total industry profits—lay in the operating system software. Bill's alliance with IBM settled the issue. After that one move, Bill Gates was set on a course that would make him the planet's richest person.

Hindsight is, of course, a wonderful thing. It is easy to say that IBM should have realized Microsoft had far more to gain than IBM from an alliance. IBM was focused on its own agenda, not that of its partners. If it had insisted on buying a large share in Microsoft as a condition of the alliance, Bill could not have refused. Perhaps Microsoft was too small a corporation for such a stupendously successful company to bother with.[6]

The story of Bill is atypical only in the scale of the consequences. Time and time again—as the behavior of Allied Domecq in selling Plymouth Gin to 80/20 people also shows—large, mature, and well-run companies do deals with small ventures that are hugely more favorable to the latter. Large and successful companies seem to love being exploited by small and new ones.

The story of Rachel

Our friend Rachel uses other firms for a majority of the product and service that her firm provides. Design is executed by individual designers and small outside firms. Manufacturing is all done by third parties. Selling in the department stores is the preserve of Rachel's people, although the stores themselves are owned and operated by other firms. Rachel has limited her operations to the conception and orchestration of the system, and to direct contact with customers.

Rachel could have done this for herself, with her own firm. The only important thing her employer "gave" her was the brand with which she started. Yet, as the Plymouth Gin experience shows, it might have been possible for her to acquire and build on a dying brand. Even the brand might not have been necessary—she has built three others from scratch.

Rachel agrees: "What I needed at the time from my company was the security and confidence that came from being part of a big company. Yet I knew even then, that if I wanted to do things, it was best not to rely on [that company's] resources or its ways of doing things. I knew I had to build a small team of people and that we had to rely on ourselves, and on deals we could strike with outside firms. So yes, I suppose we were exploiting other firms. And yes, I suppose we could have done it on our own account—if we had had the confidence."

The pursuit of growth

Over-capacity is not the only reason for large, mature companies to seek alliances with younger and smaller ones. The other main reason is lack of growth.

If we exclude acquisitions, almost no Fortune 50 company has ever grown at more than 5 percent per annum.[7] It seems that size and growth are incompatible.

No wonder large firms want to enter strategic alliances with smaller ventures. Many of these will be good for both sides, but 80/20 people are likely to benefit more.

In the early days of LEK Consulting, when we were short of clients, we entered into an alliance with PA Consulting, a large, old-established firm. The deal was simple. PA used its network to provide leads and introduce us to clients. As part of the family, PA clients were more disposed to use us. In return, we gave PA half the profits earned and a new high-growth product line.

It worked reasonably well. Although PA only "gave" us a few clients, they tended to be large, long, and profitable engagements. However, there was a flaw for PA. Over time LEK, which retained its own brand, became stronger and less dependent on PA. As we were growing very fast anyway, the constraint on growth became internal—our ability to coach and train good professional staff—rather than external. Beyond a certain time, what PA provided was not worth the profits it took. When we ended the relationship with PA, we kept all of "its" clients.

The moral of the story? Do open-ended deals with larger corporations, one where you can review their contribution versus their take. In general, the new venture gains more to start with than later on. For this reason, the large corporation should try to negotiate an equity stake in the venture. But 80/20 people should refuse this poisoned chalice, insisting instead on a deal based on a share of revenues or profits that can be easily terminated.

Alliances are useful, but they do not have to be for ever. Get engaged but not married.

How to enlist other firms

1 Identify missing ingredients in missing markets

While thinking about which new business to launch, reflect on the large companies you know and try to think of the missing ingredients that have eluded them. Mature companies often possess nine-tenths of the puzzle: They have brands, manufacturing assets, and access to markets, but they lack the imagination to unlock the total answer. If you can find the small missing piece of the jigsaw, you have a ready-made venture.

Economists talk about "missing markets." What they mean is that opportunities may be real and recognized, but no one takes the initiative to start an enterprise to fill the gap.[8] Only individuals can do this.

Individuals have local knowledge that can be the basis of a new business. Most often, however, this information is not exploited, because individuals do not form a business around their insights. As the great Austrian economist F.A. Hayek explained in 1945, because local knowledge is not exploited fully, the economy does not grow nearly as fast as it could:

"The peculiar character of the problem of a rational economic order is ... that the knowledge of the circumstances of which we must make use never exists in concentrated or integrated form, but solely as the dispersed bits of incomplete and frequently contradictory knowledge which all the separate individuals possess. The economic problem of society is ... how to secure the best use of resources known to any of the members of society ... it is a problem of the utilization of knowledge not given to anyone in its totality."[9]

It is up to you to add your local knowledge to the raw materials of business that are already available in large, mature corporations.

In the case of Plymouth Gin, my partners knew how to revive a defunct brand. Whether the brand managers within Allied Domecq had these skills or not, they did not want to use them. There was a missing market. My partners had the missing ingredient. The market is missing no more.

The second and third hotels acquired by Zoffany Hotels came from a respected hotel chain, Trust House Forte. It sold them cheaply because it could not make them work. Trust House Forte operated around a central reservation system for bookings, and there was not enough central demand for these two locations, which were small towns with no tourist trade. The missing ingredient here was simple: local marketing of the hotel to business users. Zoffany trains its managers to scour the local business community for business. Measured by return on sales and return on capital, these hotels are now two of the most profitable in England.

Think how much more attractive it would be for you to take a ready-made solution from one or more existing corporations than to start something from scratch. The ingredients are there in other firms. It is just like having a packet soup: Instead of water, you add an idea or a skill that is missing.

Take a new page. On the left side, write down all the large organizations you know well. In the middle, identify where they have missing markets: businesses they could have but don't, or businesses they do have that are not profitable. On the right, identify in each case the missing ingredient. If the missing ingredient is something you have or could appropriate from elsewhere—maybe by inviting a new partner into your consortium—then you have a ready-made new venture.

If this does not trigger a new business idea, take a second page. Write down all the ingredients—unusual insights, skills, or assets—that you and your team possess. Then try to find an existing large firm, or several, that lacks these ingredients but otherwise has the raw material for a new venture. To be a valid case, the ingredients supplied by the other firm or firms must comprise a majority of the activity in the new venture, but your ingredient alone must make it viable and highly profitable.

When you have a shortlist of such firms, approach them to see if they will provide the materials you need, either by renting them to you for a fee (a royalty or revenue-sharing arrangement), or by selling them to you, or by entering a joint venture (to share profits or equity). Generally, the order in which I have arranged the options is the order of desirability: It is better to rent than to buy, because this lowers risk and preserves capital, and better to buy than to joint venture, because the latter sacrifices a share of profits.

In making your approach to the other firm, work out how you can help it and position your proposition in these terms of the benefit to it. There is no need to point out that it will help your fledgling business many times more than you will help it. You always have other options.

2 Adhere strictly to the 80/20 parsimony principle

The 80/20 parsimony principle says: Only undertake activities with a very high return on capital and on 80/20 people's effort.

If an activity has a low return, you should not perform it. Ideally, don't provide it at all. If your customers insist on a bundled purchase, outsource the activity to another firm.

Even if an activity appears to be very profitable, it may still be better to outsource it, if the activity absorbs energy that could be better used to generate even higher profits.

To have a place in the sun, you'll need to provide some unique products or services to your customers. The activities provided should all be highly profitable: the 20 percent or less of effort that realizes at least 80 percent of rewards. In these activities, your firm must be very different from all possible competitors—and far more popular with your customers.

The danger is that you will do too much and engage other firms to do too little. Remember that it is more difficult to stop doing something than it is never to do it in the first place.

The two best "choke points" to prevent activity arising are capital and labor. Scrutinize every point at which capital or employees are to be used. Ask whether it would not be better to use another firm—to use someone else's capital or labor. Only if the activity concerned is highly profitable, and if a lower-cost alternative does not exist (or would compromise your franchise with customers), should you agree to use your own capital or employees.

It used to be that new ventures always required more capital and more people than they originally planned. Now, whenever I look at a business plan, I reduce the amount of capital and the number of employees to 25 percent of the original level proposed, while not reducing revenues or profits. Think whether each activity is necessary, or whether other firms should do it for you.

Go on as you mean to start. Whenever anyone tenders for an increase in headcount or capital, ask whether the need is highly profitable and, even if it is, whether there isn't more profit in fulfilling it externally.

3 Separate drones from star partners, one-offs from permanent deals
There are two types of transactions with third parties. There is the one-off deal, such as buying Plymouth Gin from Allied Domecq. Then there is the permanent deal, such as the 50/50 venture between Plymouth Gin and Vin & Sprit.

For one-off deals the quality of the partner does not matter. The bargain is done and then over.

Resist permanent alliances initially. Start with looser deals, from which you can easily and elegantly extricate yourself. Do not sell equity unless you really have to, or unless the other party can very clearly add long-term as well as short-term benefits.

For permanent alliances the quality of the partner is vital. Expect a skewed distribution: fewer than 20 percent of possible partners are likely to provide 80 percent of the possible value to you.

Wherever possible, for the later category, ensure that you take the initiative in selecting the partner firm. Otherwise, how can you be sufficiently selective? If you are approached by another firm proposing a joint venture, make an exhaustive list of all possible substitute firms. One will probably be much better.

There is clearly an intermediate area, where a deal may last for a fixed period and be renewable by mutual consent. If you intend the deal to last for ever, behave as if it will.

4 Force birds of a different feather together
If growth ultimately derives from individuals, this is true in other firms as well as in your own. As always, a large majority of growth or potential growth—for which you and your team are the catalyst—will derive from a few of these individuals in the firm or firms with which you collaborate.

Finding these individuals is hard but worth it. Then you have to motivate them. Don't assume that they share your obsession with profits.

As my Dutch partner Pieter says: "In dealing with the managers inside
[another firm], when we started, we went about it the wrong way. We
thought that they would be turned on by the profit opportunity. Then
we realized that what they liked more was top-line growth. In fact, we
discovered, it wasn't really the financial side at all. They liked being part
of a growth project. They had seen and enjoyed being part of an earlier
mega-growth story, and they wanted to do the same thing again. They
liked the excitement, the advertising campaigns, the glitz, and the
momentum. It was as simple as that."

If the managers in other firms are not that interested in the profits, it
actually widens the range of motivation that you can deploy, and means
that you may be able to extract the great majority of gain from any activity. Identify their "hot buttons." Perhaps all they want is a pleasant new
challenge and a sense of shared achievement. It is important that the individuals you co-opt like you, and see your project as theirs as well.

Individuals have different insights and access to different resources.
Birds of a feather flock together, yet business opportunity comes when
birds of a different feather are forced together.

The need to attain local knowledge of different types requires individuals to be linked to distant and different people. This is the "power of
weak ties," where a large number of infrequent and shallow relationships
between individuals from disconnected groups is more valuable than
connections that do not have such diversity and access to different
resources.[10]

Layer into this the insight from the 80/20 principle—that in any con-
ceivable total of relationships between individuals, a select few of them
will contain most of the value—and you have a potent brew for innovation. Before you start your venture, look far and wide for individuals
whose local knowledge is different than yours, but fantastically complementary. Delay your launch until you have found the match made in
heaven.

What 80/20 people can do

80/20 people are lucky. Large and mature firms are more willing than ever to do things for new or small ventures. The larger and older firms are driven by excess capacity and by the realization that growth is easier across rather than within their corporate boundaries.

80/20 people:

❖ Are ultra-selective in the activities they undertake—they stick to what is super-profitable and super-simple.
❖ Use other firms to do most of their work.
❖ Provide the "missing link" to unlock huge hidden value.
❖ Enlist the right firms.
❖ Search out the right individuals, with the right chemistry, in these firms. Success flows from a few individuals in the right place, at the right time, with the right mix of different local knowledge.

Notes and references

1   Karl Marx and Friedrich Engels (1848) *The Communist Manifesto*, Chapter 1. I am quoting from the translation by Samuel Moore, first published in 1888, and from the edition with Introduction and Notes by A. J. P. Taylor (1967, 1985), Penguin Books, p. 86. Marx argues that the conquest of new markets will not create enough demand for the new productive forces of industry, and that there will be progressively more extensive and destructive crises. This did not happen, because the "proletarians" and other poor people eventually provided the market that industry needed. The same redemptive process has happened in every country where free markets have been allowed to operate, and can happen in every poor country that still exists.

2   Larry Shulman (2000) *The End of the Public Company—As We Know It*, The Boston Consulting Group, Boston. This is one of BCG's excellent series of "Perspectives." Mr. Shulman may be contacted at: shulman.larry@bcg.com. It is ironic that a firm of business consultants that advocates free markets and free enterprise so eloquently should return to Marx's argument after a gap of one and a half centuries. Marx was wrong, but Mr. Shulman is right.

3   *Ibid.*

4   *Ibid.*: "The globalization wave in many traditional industries is driven more by this specific financial logic than by any compelling strategic imperative. In effect, companies are using their excess cash to take other companies private, thus liquidating the shareholders of the acquired company rather than their own."

5   As late as 1988, an observer at Comdex noted the ambivalence of Microsoft's booth: "While most booths focused on a single blockbuster technology, Microsoft's resembled a Middle Eastern bazaar. In one corner, the company was previewing the second version of Windows ... in another, it touted its latest release of DOS. Elsewhere, it was displaying OS/2 ...[and] major new releases of Word, Excel ...[and] SCO Unix. 'What am I supposed to make of all this?' grumbled a corporate buyer standing next to me." See Eric D. Beinhocker (1999) "On the origin of strategies," *McKinsey Quarterly*, 4, pp. 47–57.

6   In the 1980s IBM's profits averaged between $8 billion and $9 billion per annum. In 1990 IBM made over $10 billion. No firm has ever equaled such profits.

7   See Donald L. Laurie (2001) *Venture Catalyst: The Five Strategies for Explosive Corporate Growth*, Nicholas Brealey, London/Perseus Publishing, Cambridge, MA. The Corporate Strategy Board and Hewlett-Packard analyzed the Fortune 50 and found that 91 percent of companies reaching that top group saw their growth drop from previous levels of 9–29 percent down to 3–4 percent. The study also showed that once companies reach the Fortune 10, they always stall. Earnings growth has to come from mergers or margin improvement.

8   P. R. Milgrom and J. Roberts (1992) *Economics, Organization, and Management*, Prentice Hall, Englewood Cliffs, NJ.

9   F. A. Hayek (1945) "The use of knowledge in society," *American Economic Review*, 35 (4), pp. 519–30.

10 See M. Granovetter (1973) "The strength of weak ties," *American Journal of Sociology*, 78 (6), pp. 1360–80.

10 *Enlist Capital*

"It's true we don't have much money so what we have to do is think."
Professor Ernest Rutherford, the man who split the atom[1]

80/20 people have always exploited capital. 80/20 people have been the few who started with a little capital—usually not their own—and ended with a cornucopia of cash.

The story of Christoforo

Raising the starting capital has never been easy. The patron saint of 80/20 people is Christoforo Colombo (1446–1506), the person in history who created the most value with the least capital.

Colombo was convinced that three small ships were all he needed to discover a westward route to the Indies. But he spent much longer trying to raise the money than on the voyage itself.

Being an Italian, he tried to raise money from Italian princes. He had the choice of many sponsors, since Italy had dozens of separate kingdoms and courts. Accordingly, he traipsed across Italy, outlining his plans to King This and Count That. They all thought his project was stupid.

He then became a subject of the duke of Anjou in France. Capital requisition refused again.

He switched his allegiance to the king of Portugal. Another rejection slip.

He presented his plan to the duke of Medina-Sedonia. Same result.

Next he tried the count of Medina-Celi. No dice. A crazy scheme.

Then the king and queen of Spain, who also said no, but more politely.

Not one to give up easily, Colombo's luck finally turned when in 1492 he witnessed the fall of Granada, the Moors' stronghold, to the Spanish forces. Realizing that Queen Isabella would be in a good mood, he tried again. Success at last! Ten weeks after setting sail, Colombo kissed the ground and named it San Salvador.[2]

Three lessons from the story of Christoforo

If your project will change the world, and have a very high return on capital, you don't take "no" for an answer.

One less obvious but equally valuable message is that capital is not really a commodity and never has been. Capital is not like the European Community's wine lake, ready to be drawn off by thirsty enterprises. Capital belongs to capitalists, so 80/20 people need to enlist other individuals. Each will have their own idiosyncrasies and criteria.

Christoforo's third lesson is that capital itself obeys the 80/20 principle. A few uses of capital are super-productive.

Capital is always lying about, as close to idle as makes no difference. Colombo's project required a tiny fraction of the wealth available in hundreds of European courts of the time. What created massive wealth for Colombo, for Spain, and for the world, was the idea and one person's commitment to make it happen, not the capital.

A tiny minority of capital creates a large majority of wealth. The multiplying factors are the idea and 80/20 people. For two centuries, Spain lived off its investment in Colombo's ships. Any two-bit count willing to have a flutter could have done the same, casually diverting the course of history.

A few big hits create wealth for society

Before modern times, the world's stock of wealth stagnated. Annual economic growth was close to zero. This was because wealth was applied to pursuits without any net economic payoff to society: to conspicuous consumption by the state and the aristocracy, to war or religion (often the same thing, as in the Crusades), to lawsuits, or to building castles or wonderful gardens. Most of these projects were wasteful, some were of priceless aesthetic value to posterity, but none made the economy grow. Wealth changed hands but did not accumulate.

The economy began to grow from the fourteenth century on, when a minority of wealth was applied to trade and technology, and hence to the development of industry. Projects like Colombo's, and those of all other traders, consumed a small proportion of Europe's available capital, yet led to nearly all economic growth. The returns on the successful projects were enormous.

When we say that the economy grows at 2 percent a year, it does not mean that every business or every household experiences a 2 percent growth rate. Some businesses will have shrunk, others will have grown at 20 percent, 50 percent, or even 100 percent. Most of the growth comes from a minority of businesses, those that are growing very fast. The businesses themselves contain many products and many projects, most of which have low or negative growth but a few of which are mushrooming. When we get below the averages, we find that it is a few points of fantastic growth that are contributing most of society's overall growth rate.

Capital is the same. Some projects have returns in the hundreds or thousands of percents. Most have low or negative returns. Wealth accumulates through the few very productive projects, and by allocating more capital to the most productive users: 80/20 people.

Capital is now less of a barrier to 80/20 people

Although today's financiers are sometimes as blind as the duke of Anjou, the duke of Medina-Sedonia, the count of Medina-Celi, and the financial advisers to the massed ranks of all the kings, dukes, counts, and lesser nobles of Italy, I have qualified good news for 80/20 people.

It is now easier to get capital than ever before. More is being allocated to new enterprise. Also, nowadays less capital is necessary to launch successfully a business of any given size or profit potential.

Under the Roman Empire, the economy was not organized in such a way as to reward investment in technological projects. The Roman Empire, like nearly all pre-modern societies, rewarded military, political, and agricultural prowess, and, in its declining years, skill in advancing religion.

The essence of modern capitalism is not the existence and proliferation of capital, but its application to trade and technology, and to business generally, where a small amount of capital can have a relatively great effect.

Throughout history, 20 percent of capital has always produced more than 80 percent of cash returns—when the capital concerned is applied to high-return business projects. However, now the absolute level of investment in business ventures is higher than ever, and so too is global growth.

Productivity growth has become less dependent on large amounts of capital. For centuries, growth in the economy required heavy investment. Investment required capital. In the mid-nineteenth century, Karl Marx invented capitalism—the economy revolved around capital.

From about 1850 to 1970, in every country whether capitalist, socialist, or communist, the importance of capital grew, yet things grew tougher for the individual entrepreneur. Big was beautiful. This was the age of the large public company, of the large organization. Capital was the scarce resource, and capital agglomerated within large corporations.

Funding any particular big business corporation was beyond the means of the individual and his family. Whereas most business activity in the nineteenth century took place in medium-sized, national, family-financed and family-run enterprises, in the twentieth century most business was transacted through large, multinational, publicly financed corporations, run by managers who were not owners. The entrepreneur was less important than the manager; the individual less important than the corporation.

Many astute and sympathetic observers thought that the entrepreneur was doomed. The great economist Joseph Schumpeter, writing in 1942, virtually penned an elegy for the entrepreneur:

> *"The essential point to grasp is that in dealing with capitalism we are dealing with an evolutionary process ... a fundamental change is upon the capitalist process ...*
>
> *"The social function [of the entrepreneur] is already losing importance and is bound to lose it at an accelerating rate ... innovation itself is being reduced to routine. Technological progress is increasingly becoming the business of trained specialists who turn out what is required and make it work in predictable ways. The romance of earlier commercial enterprise is rapidly wearing away ...*
>
> *"The perfectly bureaucratized giant industrial unit not only ousts the small or medium-sized firm and 'expropriates' its owners, but also the entrepreneur ... and the bourgeoisie as a class ... stands to lose not only its income but also what is infinitely more important, its function."*[3]

So the barrier to the twentieth-century entrepreneur was capital and its increasing concentration in large corporations. However, capitalism has evolved yet again, perhaps beyond the stage where "capitalism" is a useful description. (Those who, like me, support free enterprise, should be willing to give up Marx's anachronistic label.) The increasing power of the 80/20 principle means that capital has become detached from its previous association with large-scale corporations.

The link between capital investment and growth has been smashed

Individual capital providers and 80/20 people have allied to produce higher returns than those available in conventional, publicly listed corporations. Capitalists have looked for the few investments with the highest returns. The proof is the large-scale emergence, since 1970, of venture capital and private equity. Although a minority of capital is still devoted to private rather than public equity, private equity has enjoyed much higher returns.

It used to be true that growth was related to physical stuff. New companies located near to their sources of raw material, or to that powering their machines. Until the last 30 years, it was commonly assumed that growth in the economy required a similar growth in physical goods and hence in capital. As a young management consultant in the later 1970s, I recall wading through masses of import and export statistics, which were always listed both in value and in weight.

The march of the 80/20 principle has left weight behind. Today, no one cares about the weight of trade. Federal Reserve Board chairman Alan Greenspan estimates that the weight of US GDP today is about the same as in 1900, yet its value has multiplied 20 times.

Things, physical things, are capital intensive. Heavy industry is capital intensive. Light industry is less so, services hardly at all. For each dollar of sales, 20 percent less capital is needed than was the case 25 years ago. As a result, about $530 billion less capital is needed.

The 80/20 principle has smashed the link between capital investment and economic growth. Between 1994 and 2000, US productivity grew by 2.8 percent a year, much higher than usual. Over half of the growth came from information technology (IT), which is not capital intensive. The capital stock of IT is less than 1 percent of total US capital stock. This is a greater than 50/1 relationship, an extreme form of the 80/20 principle.

Growth in today's economy is not greatly driven by capital, but by technology, ideas, and 80/20 people. Technology has freed itself from capital. Economist Lester Thurow avows, "Without his furnace, Bessemer could not have made steel."[4] 80/20 people no longer need such expensive tools.

The terms of trade between capital and entrepreneur have swung in our favor. Yet everyone still over-estimates the value of capital, and under-estimates that of really powerful ideas and 80/20 people.

In generating wealth today, it is not capital that matters, but a small nucleus of capital coated with a large outer ring of powerful ideas and initiative, pursued by individuals. Not capital, but capital plus: capital + ideas; capital + 80/20 people.

Two reasons for caution

First, it may be easier than ever before to raise capital, but it is still difficult. Having been on both sides of the funding fence in the past dozen years, I know that the capital provider has more power than the venture provider.

Second, 80/20 people nearly always need some capital, usually more than they expect!

Most new firms go bust, always because they run out of cash. The worst time to try to raise money is not at the start. It is when you've been funded, but have run out of cash.

How to enlist capital

1 Use capital only where you can multiply it

Each dollop of capital you use should be turned into three or more dollops within a few years. 20 percent of capital produces 80 percent of returns. 80 percent of capital produces 20 percent of returns. You don't want any of your capital to be in this latter 80 percent.

Will you multiply capital? Take your business plan and see what the total return to capital will be. For example, if you raise $1 million of capital, will you to able to return at least $3 million of capital when the business is sold?

This is the "cash-to-cash" ratio used by venture capitalists. They like to see a cash-to-cash ratio of at least three times, preferably five, ten, or higher.

The other test that venture capitalists apply is the "internal rate of return" or IRR. This daunting phrase simply means the average compound percentage return to capital over the years it is used. For example, if you use $1 million of capital and it takes one year to turn it into $3 million, this would be an IRR of 200 percent (the profit would be $2 million, double the starting stake). If it took three years to turn $1 million into $3 million, the IRR would be 44 percent.

You need a computer or fancy calculator to calculate the IRR, but you can check it by multiplying it out as follows:

Year 1	$1.00m × 1.44 = $1.44m
Year 2	$1.44m × 1.44 = $2.07m
Year 3	$2.07m × 1.44 = $3.00m.

For a new business, a venture capitalist may require a 50 percent IRR. You can work out for each year the total return needed to justify this:

Year 1	$1.00m × 1.5 = $1.5m
Year 2	$1.50m × 1.5 = $2.25m
Year 3	$2.25m × 1.5 = $3.38m
Year 4	$3.38m × 1.5 = $5.06m

and so on.

The total return on your new business plan may not be satisfactory. Say it reveals over three years a cash-to-cash ratio of two times, which is an IRR of only 26 percent. Divide your business up as many different ways as you can: by product, by channel, by customer or customer type, by geography, by technology used. Examine the return on capital—the cash-to-cash and IRR ratios—for each split.

For example, you find that the return over the three-year period is as follows:

Product A uses $0.5m of capital and returns $0.75m

Product B uses $0.25m of capital and returns $1.5m

Product C uses $0.25m of capital and returns −$0.25m

The ratios for the three products are therefore:

	Cash-to-cash ratio	Internal rate of return
Product A	1.5 times	14%
Product B	6 times	82%
Product C	0.25 times	Negative
Total/average	2 times	26%

You would clearly decide to forget about Products A and C, and build a business around Product B.

Always analyze the returns for each lump of capital used. A tighter focus will make you richer.

2 Reduce your need for capital

Reducing the need for capital does not mean reducing the size or upside from your new venture. The way to reduce your need for capital is to use that of other firms. Limit your activities, not your ambitions.

For every dollar of cost you have, you should normally have two or more dollars of external cost; in other words, at least two-thirds of your costs should be bought-in goods and services. This way, the majority of "real" capital you use will never figure in your books. Export at least two-thirds of your capital need, preferably three-quarters.

3 Raise more capital than you need

If capital is expensive, is this dumb? Nope.

1 percent of capital can cause you 99 or 100 percent of damage. The 1 percent is the capital you don't have, which forces you under.

Since new ventures are inherently unpredictable, don't believe your plan. Cut the amount of capital you need by structural policy decisions, by tight focus and outsourcing. But then allow yourself a very generous margin of error in estimating your need for capital. Raise $1.5 million of capital for every $1 million you think you need.

4 Provide your own capital

The proof that capital is not a commodity is that its price varies enormously. 20 percent of capital will have more than 80 percent of the cost.

80/20 people think very hard about where to get capital and what it costs.

Here are the main sources of capital, ranked from cheapest to most expensive:

- Capital made unnecessary by other firms (outsourcing).
- Suppliers and other creditors, and billing customers in advance (negative working capital).
- Your own savings.
- Capital from family and friends.
- Bank debt.
- Capital from your existing employer.
- Capital from alliances with other firms.
- Public equity (from floating on the stock market).
- Angel equity (from rich individuals).
- Specialist industry sources of finance (e.g., insurance companies).
- Private equity (for developing businesses).
- Venture capital (for new businesses).

Near the top of the list are your own savings. Make it an iron rule to save 20 percent of your income. You can always save 20 percent.

5 Use the cheapest available sources of external capital

Use other firms' capital through outsourcing, and as much capital from suppliers and other creditors as you can. Use customers' money by charging them in advance; sympathetic clients are surprisingly willing to do this for a new business, while consumers can often be induced to pay for a service in advance (for example in subscriptions or service contracts). When I was a management consultant, we changed the rules by asking for fees before we undertook the work; we were rarely refused.

Capital from family and friends will generally be cheaper and less onerous than that from third parties. Friends and family are more likely to be able to help than they were a generation ago. Longer business cycles and higher stock markets have put spare cash into many more pockets.

Bank debt may also be quite cheap, generally 1–3 percent above bank rates, although you generally have to give the security of your assets, probably your house. If the business fails and you lose your home, the loan may turn out to be horribly expensive. If at all possible—and it often is—get bank debt secured on the assets of the business you are buying, not on your personal possesssions.

A joint venture with your existing employer will be particularly tempting if that firm is willing to provide the new capital required. "Internal" capital, from the employer, is much cheaper than external capital. With luck, your new venture's funds will be costed only slightly above the old firm's required rate of return (despite the much higher risk). If the internal money is cheap, it is worth taking significantly more than you think you need.

In negotiating with an existing employer, insist on you and your team receiving a chunky slug of the equity: at least one-third for the team if the old firm is providing all the cash, and more if the team is providing some cash. Also, try to cap the old firm's return—ask that beyond a certain level of return (value of the business when you sell it), 100 percent of the benefit should go to the team. You will have to settle for a lower number, but it is reasonable to argue that the team should have a disproportionate share of any mega-profits, known to venture capitalists as a "ratchet," because beyond a certain success condition the team's share ratchets up to a higher percentage.

Consider funding from "business angels," rich individuals. You are likely to secure a much better deal from individuals than from venture capital or private equity institutions.

Remember that specialist industry finance may be attractive. For example, when hotel companies wanted to expand, there used to be only three serious sources of funds: bank debt, public equity, and private equity. Now there is another opportunity: a deal with insurance companies or pension funds whereby they fund hotel acquisitions in exchange for a fixed long-term rental.

Even within the venture capital and private equity community, shop around for the best possible deal. Different houses have different views on particular industries, technologies, types of business, and management teams. Venture capital and private equity will always be expensive, but there can be staggering differences between deals offered on the same transaction.

Never confine yourself to one house as a potential funder, even if you are offered a reasonable deal. Go to three or four other houses and see what terms they are willing to offer. Even when you are close to a deal, keep another horse in the race right to the end. This is not only wise insurance; it is necessary to ensure that you don't get screwed at the last minute. Play off one source of capital against another to improve your terms.

In negotiating with venture capital professionals, remember that they have experience as well as cash on their side. You will only ever raise money once or a few times. They assess deals between meals every day. Even up the odds by hiring an experienced lawyer or corporate financier who is willing to help in the nitty-gritty deal making.

In Chapter 8 we met Sir Paul Judge, the man who arranged the £97 million buyout of Premier Brands from Cadbury Schweppes. His story is an excellent example of how to use the cheapest available external capital.

Faced with the need for this kind of money, most of us would head straight off to private equity houses. Paul had another idea. He managed to arrange £77 million of asset-backed finance from Bankers Trust and Citibank, on normal banking terms. That still left a gap of £20 million. But instead of reaching for his kneepads and the venture capital directory, Paul had a brilliant idea, now known as "Judge's gambit."

Premier had an operation called Kenco, the leader in supplying coffee to restaurants in the UK. General Foods was keen to acquire it. Kenco was worth about £15 million. Paul effectively sold this business to General Foods before he owned it, but did it in a way that gave the buyout team the full £20 million of financing they needed. Paul gave General Foods an option to buy Kenco for £9 million, in exchange for General Foods guaranteeing the final £20 million needed for the buyout. This meant that all the money for the buyout was funded at 0.5 percent over LIBOR, instead of the typical 35 percent return required each year by private equity houses.

Paul and the other directors therefore owned 100 percent of the new business, having funded the buyout without venture capital. As mentioned earlier, Paul personally made more than £40 million when Premier was sold to a trade buyer less than three years later. Had venture capitalists been involved, Paul's profit would probably have been a quarter or less of what he pocketed.

6 Be obsessed with cash

Any business venture is like Monopoly or any other cash-driven board game. You start with a small amount of cash. Your objective is to turn it into a large amount of cash. Your ability to do this is the best test of whether you are adding economic value. An obsession with cash is not just for bean counters. It is the acid test of 80/20 people, creating unusual value by adding a small amount of cash to extraordinarily powerful ideas.

Each year, examine the relationship between capital used and your cash return for each product, activity, customer, distribution channel, and region. In all cases, look for the vital few cases where returns are fantastically high. Move heaven and earth to expand this business. For the rest, raise the returns or stop allocating capital to them.

7 Treat capital providers as valued partners

Capital is not a commodity; nor are its providers. The 80/20 principle applies to capital providers too: Some are much more successful than others.

Choose successful capital providers. If they endorse your plan, that should give you confidence. If they criticize your plan, there is probably something wrong with it. In my experience, successful capital providers have intuitive skills that even they under-value. A suggested tweak to your ideas, a throw-away line here, a tentative hint there—listen carefully!

Treat your capital providers as full partners. Take your obligations seriously. Exceed every budget, target, and expectation. Even if you cannot do this, always be open and honest. If you suspect things are going wrong let them know early, not when it is too late. If your fears are groundless, you will have gained a reputation for prudence; if things really prove dicey, the unpleasant surprise will be less sudden and resonant.

In a way, the capital providers are the economy's conscience department for your venture. You start out with the aspiration of multiplying capital: the job of the 80/20 person who catches on to the coat tails of powerful business genes. If things go wrong, it is either because the business genes are not as powerful as you thought, or because you have not tied yourself to their coat tails more securely than have your rivals. The economy will only tell you whether your are succeeding or not, whether you are multiplying cash. The capital providers can help you work out why.

Keeping score

Ideas and 80/20 people drive business progress. Capital keeps the score. There is no such thing as a good business that cannot multiply capital. 80/20 people start with a very small amount of capital and end up pumping out masses of the stuff.

The paradox of the 80/20 principle is that if capital became too cheap, it would cease to perform its function.[5] 80/20 people leverage and exploit capital, but also respect its scarcity. High capital cost is the best spur to extraordinary performance. Once you feel capital is abundant, exit and start again.

We should be eternally grateful to venture capitalists, both for making capital available and for keeping its price so high.

Notes and references

1 I thank Sir Paul Judge for this reference. Rutherford uttered his remark when visited by a team of American scientists, who were amazed at his cramped work quarters at Cambridge University, England, and the poor quality of his equipment. Rutherford's point was that in splitting the atom, thinking from first principles was more important than having the latest equipment or the plushest laboratory. Ideas dominated capital.

Following the fall of communism, western physicists working with their Russian counterparts were surprised to find that the Russians had much shorter and neater algorithms. Because the Soviets had much less computer power they found ways of making it go further: more from less.

2   See Norman Davies (1996) *Europe: A History*, Oxford University Press, Oxford, and Jared Diamond (1997) *Guns, Germs and Steel: A Short History of Everybody for the Last 13,000 Years*, Chatto & Windus, London.

3   Joseph A. Schumpeter (1942) *Capitalism, Socialism and Democracy*, Harper & Row, New York.

4   Lester C. Thurow (1999) *Creating Wealth: The New Rules for Individuals, Companies and Countries in a Knowledge-Based Economy*, Nicholas Brealey, London.

5   This is what happened to gold. Once it ceased to out-perform other assets, it lost its whole rationale. Too much gold and gold was no longer golden.

11 Enlist Zigzag Progress

"Failure or success seem to have been allocated to men by their stars. But they retain the power of wriggling ... and in the whole universe the only really interesting movement is this wriggle."

E. M. Forster

The most challenging time for 80/20 people is not conceiving the business idea, nor assembling the team, nor raising the money, nor getting the business off the ground. It is once it is successful. Short of selling it immediately, what do you do to develop the business creatively so that it can fulfill its potential?

This is the difference between making a good return—perhaps multiplying the capital by five to ten times—and making a return in the ten to a thousand times range.

A venture that can make a five times return within, say, four years, should be capable of making a twenty-five times return within eight years. Over both periods, the internal rate of return is about 50 percent.

Because of ratchets, the difference in what 80/20 people pocket may be even greater. You could take $5 million, say, after four years, or $50 million after eight if the business continued to be super-successful.

Of course, it's not all about money. 80/20 people, who have given birth to a terrific new business, want to see it prosper further. They want to see their colleagues, including more recent, younger recruits, grow and get rich. They want their reputations to rest on a permanently successful addition to the economy, not on a get-rich-quick-and-sell-on-to-the-nearest-corporate-mug flash in the pan.

Is it really a success to start a company, make a go of it, and then sell it quickly?

The more successful an enterprise in its first three to five years, the greater the upside for the future—if it can maintain its upward trajectory.

There's the rub. It is not easy to keep a brilliant new venture growing at its original rate for more than three to five years. In fact, if you continue doing the same things that made you successful in the first place, you're almost certain to fail. It is easy to change when things are going badly. It is much more difficult—and hugely more important—to change when things are going well.

What can help you reach the second stage of growth?

A zigzag path to the jackpot

Progress comes from a zigzag course. To find the new vital few parts of reality on which your business is impinging—to find the new 20 percent of inputs that will yield the precious 80 percent or more of results—requires experimentation and insight.

The 80/20 principle is dynamic. It operates over time. The valuable 20 percent today may not be the vital 20 percent tomorrow. Even if it is, there is *another* even more valuable 20 percent within the vital 20 percent you already know about. There is a higher level of value, a minority within the minority. But to find this gem, you will have to wade through acres of waste. The trivial many always hide the vital few.

Evolution by natural selection

As we discussed in Chapter 4, progress in natural selection depends on reproduction, on producing a large number of new versions of successful products and activities. Most of these variations will fail. They have to be produced in large and apparently wasteful numbers because *nobody can tell in advance which variations will work in a particular time and place.*

As Charles Darwin observed:[1] "The slightest advantage in one being ... over those with which it comes into competition, or better adaptation in however slight a degree to the surrounding physical conditions, will turn the balance."

Yet natural selection can only operate when there is a change in the "conditions of life," such as climate: "[Change] would manifestly be favourable to natural selection, by giving a better chance of profitable variations occurring; and unless profitable variations do occur, natural selection can do nothing."

Successful variations in nature will live longer and reproduce more. This prolific sex life leads to more variations, most of which will be rejected by the environment. The few successes will breed extensively, and so the process goes on.

The story of Sam

Sam Walton, the founder of Wal-Mart, once said, "most everything I've done I've copied from someone else." Like most 80/20 people, Walton was a voracious copier of successful ideas, but he always applied the ideas to a new arena and with his own distinctive traits. And he always continued innovating.

Sam's basic insight was that rural and small-town America was underserved by retailers. The stores were too small and too expensive. He set about correcting this.

By the early 1960s, when he was aged 40 or so, Sam Walton had become the largest independent variety store operator in the US—and very rich. But he was not satisfied. He was always after something more, something new.

One day he took two buses, a total of 630 miles each way, to follow up a rumor. He had heard that two Ben Franklins stores, in Pipestone and Worthington, Minnesota, had a self-service system. What he found was one central checkout rather than the then universal practice of a cash register at'each counter. Self-service was cheaper, but also saved the shopper time—and increased what was spent, as attention was drawn less often to the cost of each item. Walton immediately implemented self-service in all his stores.

Despite his success, in 1960 Walton was looking for the second stage of growth. As he later wrote: "I mean, after 15 years we were only doing $1.4m in fifteen stores ... I began looking around hard for whatever new idea would break us over into something with a little better payoff for all our efforts."[2]

Walton's answer was to build large discount stores in new locations, typically small towns where nobody believed there was a sufficient market to sustain a proper discount store. Once again, note the pattern: an idea that had proved itself but a new context. Sears and the A&P had already made a fortune from discount stores. Walton took the idea and experimented in small towns.

The first Walton Family Center opened in St. Robert, Missouri, in 1962. Only 1,500 people lived there. Yet Sam opened a large store: 13,000 square feet. It was so successful that he quickly enlarged it to 20,000 square feet. Within a year, his running rate of sales was $2 million, more from one store than two years earlier from his 15 variety stores.

Sam then extended the concept, opening the first proper Wal-Mart store in Rogers, Arkansas, in July 1962, with huge placards shouting "Always the low price—Always." Sam had found his second stage of growth.

Winners should breed prolifically

In business, therefore, it is the success stories that have the greatest opportunity and obligation to produce a large number of variants of the success. Most of these variants will fail. A few of them—and it is impossible to predict in advance which few—will succeed.

If you have a successful new venture on your hands, therefore, you have a heavy responsibility to experiment extensively. That is how you get to the second stage of growth and hit the jackpot.

Yet what do we observe with new enterprises?

❖ Most new ventures rest on their laurels and do not vary the formula that has brought success. The implicit assumption is: Why tinker with the goose that lays the golden eggs? But sooner or later the formula stops working so well. It hits diminishing returns. At this stage, the growth trajectory of the business is called into question and its value plunges.

❖ An alternative outcome is that there is some experimentation, but the experiments fail, or at least are not as successful as the original formula. At this stage, the founder gets everyone together and says, in effect, "I wanted to give you young people your head. I didn't want any sacred cows around here. But the market has spoken. From now on we stick to our tried-and-tested way of doing things." Experimentation stops. The original route to success works for a time, but then it stops working so well ...

Great business pioneers often screw up the second stage of growth

In 1910, 458,000 American families had cars. Ten years later, the number was 8,225,000.[3] Henry Ford created this market and by 1920 owned most of it. Yet by 1937, Ford Motor Corporation had slumped into third place with only 21 percent market share, compared to 25 percent for Chrysler and 42 percent for General Motors.[4]

Why? Because Henry Ford, the greatest innovator of the 1900s and 1910s, refused to innovate in the 1920s and 1930s. Ford had far fewer new models and far less variety than its rivals.

I have seen this pattern so many times that I often despair. What are 80/20 people to do?

A cynical solution is to sell out at the first indication that growth is faltering. However, there is a better option. Twist the successful recipe every which way until you come up with an even more mouth-watering dish. Keep going until you have another unexpected success. Then roll that out until it stops working so well, and produce a huge number of new variants until you hit the jackpot again.

LEK Consulting: Successful variation of fantastic business genes

As I have discussed before, my first venture was as one of three founders of a strategic consulting firm. I put in a few hundred thousand dollars, out of savings, as working capital. After six years this had multiplied 24 times. We never needed all the capital, but it helped us sleep at night.

We enjoyed a fantastic heritage. First we imitated. Then we experimented. We set up an academic council to try to develop the next hot concept. This expensive initiative failed, as did many others.

Undaunted, we kept moving. We hired many inexperienced junior staff, and found that they could perform cheap and effective analysis using PCs in the office. Some of our largest clients faced hostile takeover bids. We defended them, using competitive analysis to scrutinize the bidders. Accidentally, we invented a new product and established our reputation.

Filofax: Success, failure, success, failure

Filofax was one of the emblematic success stories of the 1980s. Although it was actually quite an old company, founded in 1922, it took off in the

1980s, driven by David Collischon. A fantastic 80/20 person, he made the mistake of bringing in big-company managers, who saddled Filofax with costs it could not carry. In desperation, David turned to me for money and to my partner, Robin Field, for management.

We pursued a classic 80/20 strategy, retrenching Filofax to its few profitable products and customers. We cut prices to come much closer to those of competitors, and cut costs to allow us to make money at the new prices. Then we introduced new variants of the most successful products. Within three years, despite cutting out most of the product range, volumes had quadrupled and Filofax reached unprecedented profits.

After three years, one of our astute co-investors sold—for seven times his cost.

Robin and I didn't sell then. That was our first mistake. Our second was not to innovate. Third, we played the corporate acquisition game.

We had a public success story. Filofax's stock soared. As consultants we had seen this before. We had seen ambitious chief executives buy companies on cheaper ratings and automatically enhance the earnings of the acquiring company, even without producing any basic economic change in the company acquired. We liked this game.

We started innocently. We made six acquisitions, all closely related to the Filofax business: four were overseas personal organizer firms, plus two UK acquisitions. All were earnings enhancing and popular with the stock exchange. But we ran out of closely related companies. Our next two acquisitions were stationery companies, to which we could add little value.

It was a cynical game. Of the two diversifications, the first paid for itself within 30 months, but the second, a greetings card company and our biggest move to date, went down very badly with the financial community. It marked down our shares. But what did the stock market analysts know? We'd prove them wrong.

The greetings card acquisition was a disaster. Worse, by playing the takeover game, we took our eye off the Filofax ball. Because we failed to innovate, the growth came to an end. Our shares, which we started buying between 13p and 30p, peaked at 280p, then fell back below 150p. In

1998 we sold the company for 210p, roughly the price five years earlier.

This was a decent return, but no bonanza. The second stage of growth eluded us. We stopped experimenting.

Belgo: A great idea but the second stage of growth botched

In Chapter 6 I described the success of Belgo, the *moules et frites*, modernistic, surreal, "Belgian" restaurants. Now a confession: our failure with Belgo's sex life.

After four years we had precisely two restaurants. The second was a variation of the first and even more successful. They were big and hugely profitable, but two restaurants a chain does not make.

I knew we had to grow, we had to vary. But somehow, I couldn't persuade my working partners to produce enough novel variants. They kept investigating new sites and producing blueprints of new ideas, but none came to fruition. For a booming business, with a return on capital in the 50–100 percent range, it was embarrassing to have only two outlets. Was this really a high-growth business, with gargantuan potential?

We had the variant growth formula: what we called mini-Belgos, later opened as Bierodromes, smaller restaurants with a very large bar area. Bierodromes proved a great success, but not under our ownership.

Because my partners and I couldn't agree on the growth plan, we sold the business. It went to the stock market. I made a 17 times return on my money, my partners more. But we botched the second stage of growth.

Looking back, the solution is so simple that I can't believe I missed it. My working partners were best at design and ideas. That was their 20 percent spike. They found the job of locating new sites and getting the restaurants ready an enormous hassle (who wouldn't?).

So why didn't we bring in a new partner, the best person in the country at developing new restaurants? We could easily afford it. We had the cash flow and capital, we had the brand, we had the new formula, we had the reputation, we had the excitement, we had nearly all the ingredients necessary for the second stage of growth. This was the jackpot that got away, and all for want of the right 80/20 person.

Zoffany Hotels: The second variant is a new entrepreneurial structure

My involvement with what is now Zoffany Hotels dates back to 1993. As I write, the formula, described in Chapter 4, continues to work very well, but there must be a questionmark over its longevity. For two years we have been searching for the Zoffany Mark II formula.

Zoffany's uniqueness lies in its entrepreneurial structure. There is no middle management; the partners relate directly to the general managers of each hotel in the group. The partners coach the general managers in the Zoffany business formula. There is a continuing working relationship between the partner and the general manager, although with less partner time as the manager gains confidence.

For some time we have worried about how far we can push this set-up. We have two working partners and ten hotels. Perhaps we could go up to sixteen hotels with two partners, each keeping an eye on eight general managers. We have been offered a group of 40 hotels at an appealing price. How could we cope? Would this be expansion too far?

Maybe. But one Zoffany innovation has been to ask two of our top general managers to look after two hotels each. So far, the trial has worked wonders. We are about to give these managers three hotels each and see how far we can push this; and to give another four managers two hotels each.

Of the 40 hotels we might buy, we would sell a dozen of them and effectively leave another 20 alone for the first year. We would concentrate on the 8 hotels that currently account for about 80 percent of the profits of the 40 hotels (by coincidence, an 80/20 relationship). We would therefore have 18 hotels (the old 10 and the new 8) to run in the Zoffany way. If we can get each experienced Zoffany general manager to take two hotels, maybe we can get to the second stage of growth.

Capstone Publishing and Plymouth Gin:
The variant is internationalization

For Capstone Publishing and Plymouth Gin, we believe that the second stage of growth is to produce international variants of the existing national strategies. For this, we needed corporate partners. My Capstone stake has been sold for a tenfold return to John Wiley & Sons. Plymouth Gin has teamed up with the owners of Absolut vodka.

What will be your second stage of growth?

The time to start thinking about your second stage of growth is before the first has happened. Sure, you'll have plenty of time to change your mind. But I wish I had realized earlier how crucial the second stage would be. Don't make the same mistake!

Notes and references

1 Charles Darwin (1859) *On the Origin of Species by Means of Natural Selection; Or, the Preservation of Favoured Races in the Struggle for Life*, John Murray, London. I quote from the 1985 Penguin, London, edition edited by J. W. Burrow.

2 Sam Walton with John Huey (1993) *Sam Walton: Made in America, My Story*, Bantam Books, London, p. 53.

3 James Dalton (1926) "What Will Ford Do Next?," *Motor*, May. Numbers from graph reproduced in Thomas K. McCraw (ed.) (1997) *Creating Modern Capitalism: How Entrepreneurs, Companies, and Countries Triumphed in Three Industrial Revolutions*, Harvard University Press, Cambridge, MA, p. 283.

4 Alfred D Chandler, Jr. (1964) *Giant Enterprise: Ford, General Motors, and the Automotive Industry*, Harcourt, Brace, & World, New York, p. 4.

Conclusion to Part II

The 80/20 principle enables people to create more from less: to express their individuality, enrich the world, and lead rewarding lives, ones where they are in control and can cultivate all that is important to them as individuals. It allows them to become 80/20 people.

This can always be done. The constraint is not demand, nor technology, nor capital, nor organization. It is not social, political, or ideological. The constraint is merely individual human imagination and initiative— of which there is more than any of us dreams—and repeated experimentation based on varying already successful formulas.

What are you waiting for?

Part III

The 80/20 Revolution

12

From Capitalism to Individualism

"Nothing has been disproved faster than the concept of the 'organization man,' which was generally accepted forty years ago."

Peter Drucker[1]

There is a new way to create wealth that is better than the dominant way used in the twentieth century. Then, under the system called managerial capitalism, all serious wealth creation required a large corporation, huge dollops of capital, and a large number of managers and workers controlled by the corporation. However, now the rules have changed. The 80/20 revolution has broken out. Instead of capital and corporations driving individuals, it is the other way round. Corporations are still important, but the most successful corporations now revolve around a few individuals. The corporations are there for the benefit of the individuals. And it is the individuals, not the corporations or capital, that are the crucial ingredient in generating new wealth and growth in the economy.

Although we are not there yet, we are headed for a totally new economy, where individuals will be the big winners. The 80/20 revolution, which is leading to the new economy, is as important as the other three transitions in economic history: the agricultural revolution, the industrial revolution, and the managerial revolution. These resulted in quite different economies and societies. Over the next two decades, the same will almost certainly happen again.

To demonstrate this we need a time machine, which I just happen to have handy.

Three stops to visit history's economies

Conveniently, our time machine will only need three stops. That is because new economies don't arise very often. The alleged "new economy" of 1997–2000 turned out to be a flash in the pan, a mere electronic version of the "old" economy. In fact there have been only three new economies in history, plus the one currently emerging.

New economies only arrive when a fundamentally new and better way of creating wealth is discovered. Inevitably this leads to a new elite and new rights, which, after a struggle, set society's seal of approval on the novel arrangements.

The agricultural revolution

Our first stop is the Middle East, 7,000 to 10,000 years before Christ. Here we see the first new economy, agriculture, gradually replacing the old economy, the nomadic existence when men hunted wild animals and women gathered wild fruit and plants.[2] Growing crops and domesticating animals was a totally different proposition. In supporting a larger population and a more complex society, the rules for making and keeping wealth had to be changed. Permanent control over land, and over the people to tend it, was necessary. Hence came land rights, serfdom, and slavery; in a word, feudalism. This basic economic system, with sub-economies of war and trade layered on, persisted until modern times.[3]

The industrial revolution

Our next stop is England in the late eighteenth century. We could have stopped a few centuries earlier, in Venice or Amsterdam, to see the development of trade and banking, the precursors of capitalism. Nevertheless, since my time machine is an express rather than a stopping service, I am taking you straight to the area around Manchester where cotton mills and other factories have sprung up, capitalizing on the invention of the steam engine to create wealth in a more concentrated and productive way than agriculture. We listen to William Blake denouncing the "dark Satanic mills," but then fast forward to 1848 to see Karl Marx scribbling a remarkable tribute to industry's power and global reach:

> *"Modern industry has established the world market, for which the discovery of America paved the way. This market has given an immense development to commerce, to navigation, to communication by land. This development has, in turn, reacted on the extension of industry; and in proportion as industry, commerce, navigation, railways extended, in the same proportion the bourgeoisie [middle classes] developed, increased its capital, and pushed into the background every class handed down from the Middle Ages.*
>
> *"The bourgeoisie has ... been the first to show what man's activity can bring about. It has accomplished wonders far surpassing Egyptian pyramids, Roman aqueducts, and Gothic cathedrals; it has conducted expeditions that put in the shade all former Exoduses of nations and crusades ...*
>
> *"The need of a constantly expanding market for its products chases the bourgeoisie over the whole surface of the globe. It must nestle everywhere, settle everywhere, establish connections everywhere.*
>
> *"The bourgeoisie has through its exploitation of the world market given a cosmopolitan character to production and consumption in every country."*[4]

For the first time in history, land became less important than industry. The factory was more productive than the farm. By the middle of the

nineteenth century the new economy had produced new rules: deregu-
lation of trade at home, free trade internationally, limited liability for business corporations, and freedom of movement for labor, so that serfdom
and slavery, where they still persisted, became obvious anachronisms.

In England the symbolic victory came in 1846, when a parliament
controlled by the landed classes, but terrified of lower-class revolution,
gave way to middle-class demands for the abolition of the Corn Laws—
agricultural protection. The promotion of free trade caused an explosion
of international trade.

In America the turning points were the Revolution of 1775–6, which
proclaimed democracy, and the Civil War of 1861–5, which extended it,
tilting economic power from the agricultural South to the industrial
North.

Market capitalism produced new middle-class winners: inventors,
entrepreneurs, factory owners. The economy comprised a mass of small
producers and shopkeepers, all competing on fairly equal terms through
the market. Firms were owned and run by individual entrepreneurs and
families, and the invisible hand of the market allocated resources.

The managerial revolution

Our third and final stop is the United States in 1891. Here we witness
two enormous organizations: the Post Office, with 95,000 workers, and
the Pennsylvania Railroad, employing 110,000 people. From here on we
see organizations growing in numbers, size, and wealth, and spreading to
span the entire globe.

To make sense of the new system, we fast forward again to New York
in 1933, to see one of the most influential books of the twentieth century roll off the presses. In *The Modern Corporation and Private Property*,
Adolf Berle and Gardiner Means took American Telephone and
Telegraph as their example of the modern, gigantic public corporation:

*"With assets of almost five billion dollars, with 454,000 employees, and
stockholders to the number of 567,694, this company [American Telephone*

and Telegraph] may indeed be called an economic empire ...

"One hundred companies of this size would control the whole of American wealth ...

"The property owner who invents in a modern corporation ... sur-renders his wealth to those in control of the corporation ...[to] become merely a recipient of the wages of capital."[5]

Ownership of these mammoth corporations became anonymous and dif-fused, centered around stock exchanges. Instead of individuals owning and managing corporations, as under the old system, ownership and management were separated, in both cases going into new hands.

The old-style factory owner gave up control to managers, at the same time that he and his family could no longer fund the voracious demands of their expanding organization. The individual entrepreneur was rele-gated to the margins of the economy, his functions replaced by industrial managers, fund managers, and stock exchanges. Thus managerial capital-ism—the economy dominated by the trinity of large organizations, col-lective capital providers, and the burgeoning cadre of managers—replaced market capitalism, dominated by entrepreneurs and markets.

Why managerial capitalism and large organizations flourished

Managerial capitalism triumphed because it held the secret of economic growth: central planning to achieve strategic goals. The large corporation could take a long-term view, could plan to transform an industry, and could execute its plans through its hierarchy, employing myriad managers and workers; all things that small entrepreneurs and markets couldn't do. For example, under the market system of the 1890s there were hundreds of American car makers, run by owner-managers, turning out small numbers of expensive cars. In 1907 Henry Ford had the vision to "democratize the automobile." To do so he needed to build a huge orga-nization. By the 1920s, the Ford Motor Corporation churned out mil-lions of cars each year at a fraction of the previous price. Free markets and individual entrepreneurs could never have created cheap autos and hence a large market for them.

The twentieth-century economy grew mainly on the back of large organizations and their strategic planning. The trick rested very largely on massive investment, managerial control, mass production, standardization, and the creation of large markets through lowering costs and prices.

Because this was a better way of creating wealth than had been known before, the economy became dominated by large organizations. As the twentieth century unfolded, there was a progressive shift from owner-managed, small-scale, national or subnational enterprises, to giant national and global corporations run by professional managers and financed through the stock market.

There were four key elements in this shift to big organizations:

❖ The invisible hand of the market was replaced by the visible hand of management.[6] Large organizations "internalized" or "insourced" market activity: They made rather than bought; they integrated vertically.

❖ As a result central planning and the management hierarchy, rather than random markets, increasingly allocated resources.

❖ Ownership was separated from control, now the preserve of managers. Ownership became less important.

❖ Corporations cornered the means of production, bundling together and monopolizing the wherewithal of enterprise. If you wanted to get anything serious done in business, you had to be part of an established, large corporation, listed on one of the world's stock markets. Corporations controlled technology, brands, and access to markets, customers and capital. In large part, corporations also monopolized business talent.

In the economy dominated by organizations, managers were the great winners. The greatest growth story of the twentieth century was the number and pay of managers. The two other major beneficiaries of managerial capitalism were organized labor and organized savers, those in pension, insurance, and mutual funds, which increasingly allocated their cash to equities—stock in the giant corporations—where they could earn the highest returns. At all levels, it paid to be organized: to belong to organizations, to place oneself in their slipstream, and to follow a collective approach to making and taking wealth.

The 80/20 revolution

Since 1980 managerial capitalism has begun to come apart at the seams. The four key elements that marked the transition to managerial capitalism have all gone sharply into reverse:

❖ Instead of insourcing from markets, large corporations have started to outsource to markets. They buy rather than make. The best-run and best-placed corporations are specializing in the things that they alone can do better than any other corporation, and shifting less demanding and lower-return activities on to other corporations.

❖ Central planning and management hierarchy are *passé*. Increasingly markets are allocating resources, as contractual relationships often prove more efficient and flexible than extensive hierarchies. The long reach of the single corporation is being replaced by many smaller and more focused—although not necessarily less profitable or valuable—enterprises.

❖ More and more, ownership and control are being reunited. Personal ownership by individuals is becoming important again, and the key individuals both run their corporations and own large and valuable stakes in them. The billionaire business magnate is back with a vengeance.

❖ The listed corporation's monopoly on the means of wealth creation is being smashed by the spontaneous actions of myriad entrepreneurs and venture capitalists. You no longer need a large, established corporation to create spectacular wealth. Instead, you can start your own firm, separately obtaining technology, brands, market access, customers, and capital from specialist third parties. Although some capital is required, the need for massive physical infrastructure and investment is much reduced. Not only can you often use established corporations' excess infrastructure, but also the amount of investment required is frequently trivial relative to the value that can be created. As I write Microsoft, the world's third most valuable corporation, is worth $286 billion. Its original external capital need was less than $100,000, well below the level at which stock markets are relevant. In 1986 Microsoft went public, raising a wholly unnecessary $44 million. When you get a return of 6,800 times the 1986 capital, or more than three million times the original capital, you know that capital is not the decisive factor.

Just as in the three earlier economic revolutions, a superior, novel way of making money has been discovered. The new way follows the 80/20 principle: to focus on the few very powerful forces operating in any arena, and especially to focus on the most productive ideas and individuals.

The old way was to aggregate. The new way is to divide, to take averages apart and concentrate on the small parts of the system that have extraordinary power to generate wealth.

The old way was to add assets and management structure. The new way is to subtract, compress, flatten, and simplify.

The old way was to piece together an intricate new big picture. The new way is to break up the jigsaw, appropriating the few most valuable parts, twisting them into a new and richer pattern. The 80/20 revolution, following the 80/20 principle, divides markets and the means of serving them into a much larger number of smaller and separate markets, niches, and activities. The new revolution involves a relentless search for the most profitable customers, products, technologies, suppliers, employees, partners, and ways of doing business.

The old way was capitalism, a system revolving around capital and large corporations with massive appetites for capital. The new way revolves around individuals; capital and corporate structures are relatively unimportant. Individualism is replacing capitalism.

If you doubt this, look at the numbers. You would expect that if capital were less important, its rate of return would fall. That is precisely what has happened. US Federal Reserve Board figures show that the return on capital, now a paltry 4.1 percent, has been falling steadily since the early 1950s. The latest peak was 1996, and even then the return was much lower than in the 1950s and early 1960s. Also, the share of profits in the economy has fallen from nearly 20 percent in the 1950s to under 8 percent today. Where is the money released going? To individuals.

Just as before, this economic revolution brings a new group of people to the top. The most successful players of the past decade are quite different to those who went before. In place of the gray and reclusive organization men who ruled in the 1950s, 1960s, 1970s, and most of the 1980s, we have colorful, idiosyncratic, boisterous, daring superstars—people such as Jeff Bezos, Richard Branson, Warren Buffett, Larry Ellison, Bill Gates, Andy Grove, Steve Jobs, Anita Roddick, George Soros, and Oprah Winfrey. The new superstars are creators, not inheritors; founders, not followers; entrepreneurs, not managers. They are also very, very rich, and influential to boot. Is it coincidental, for instance, that capital gains taxes have plummeted at precisely the same time that the billionaire superstars have ascended?

The new breed of corporation

Perhaps the most seminal change in the transition to a new economy has already happened. The fact is that the most successful corporations of recent years revolve around a few key individuals. Firms such as Amazon, Apple, Berkshire Hathaway, Goldman Sachs, Hewlett-Packard, Microsoft, Oracle, Virgin, and Wal-Mart are personal vehicles for their top executives, who are usually the founders and a few close associates. These corporations serve the individuals, not the other way round. The corporations embody the vision and values of their 80/20 leaders and are platforms for their self-expression.

There is also a high correlation between the success of the corporations and the wealth of their top people, because they have large equity stakes in the firms they run. For several years the world's richest two people have been Warren Buffett and Bill Gates, based on the extraordinary run of success enjoyed by Berkshire Hathaway and Microsoft. In the Fortune 500 list for 2001, Bill Gates' 12.3 percent stake in Microsoft was

worth \$35 billion, while the value of Warren Buffett's 31.2 percent of
Berkshire Hathaway—some \$32 billion—was almost as mind-boggling.
The only comparable personal wealth in America is the \$81.6 billion
shared by five Walton family directors of Wal-Mart, another individual-
centered corporation (the directors own 40 percent of the company).[7]

There have, of course, always been entrepreneurs such as Andrew
Carnegie, Henry Ford, John and Forrest Mars, John D. Rockefeller, and
Sam Walton, all of whom dominated their corporations and became
hugely rich through their success. Yet not since the late 1930s has such a
significant chunk of stock market value accrued to corporations that
were personal vehicles run principally by and for the benefit of the
founders and their coteries.

In 1933, Adolf Berle and Gardiner Means made their names by discovering that two-thirds of America's large corporations were run by
salaried managers rather than entrepreneurs. Had they computed the
market value of these companies, they would have found that a large
majority of that, too, belonged to what was then the new breed of publicly owned corporation. In 2001, traditional corporations still accounted
for a substantial majority of US stock market value. Yet even at the very
top, in the elite club of the 20 most valuable corporations, there are these
three individual-centered companies: Berkshire Hathaway, Microsoft, and
Wal-Mart.

I define an individual-centered corporation as one where at least one
key executive personally owns more than 10 percent of the shares, or
where employees collectively own more than 15 percent. All three companies happen to satisfy both conditions. A more liberal definition of the
individual-centered corporation—where the directors own more than 5
percent—would lead us to include AOL Time Warner as well as the other
three companies. My rule for defining individual-centered corporations
is quite stringent. If we were to include all companies where an executive has become a billionaire, regardless of percentage ownership, the list
would be much longer.[8]

Do these individual-centered corporations truly represent the wave of
the future? They may be much more profitable, more focused, need much

less capital, and make better use of it. Yet a tally of three or four individual-centered corporations out of America's 20 most valuable may not represent an inevitable trend. There were none ten years ago; you had to go down to number 48 in the 1990 Fortune 500 list—Apple Computer—to find an individual-centered corporation. Does this mean that in ten years' time there will be eight or ten such corporations in the Fortune 20? Or twenty? Or zero?

The argument cannot be settled statistically. What intrigues me, however, is that the most successful "traditional" organizations—those that have been trading a very long time and where the top executives are not founders—have tended in recent years to be those that approximate most to the new breed of corporation. Think of General Electric's remarkable and prolonged resurgence under Jack Welch, which took it to the top of the Fortune ranking. Or of the Coca-Cola Corporation, which enjoyed terrific success under Robert Goizueta, making him a billionaire in the process. These corporations were not set up as personal vehicles for 80/20 people, yet they became, for a time, something rather similar.

What is extraordinary is how individual-centered corporations have already reached into the top drawer of US corporate life. Gaining a foothold at the pinnacle is, of course, very much more difficult for individual founders than is being successful below this level. In the rest of the Fortune 500, in smaller listed corporations, and in a huge number of private corporations and partnerships, we are witnessing a massive renaissance of individual enterprise, with rewards increasingly going to visionary individuals who turn existing structures and ideas upside down and create new growth. The 80/20 revolution is transforming business, literally from top to bottom.

What is really new about individual-centered corporations?

Is "all" we are seeing a reversion to the typical nineteenth-century business, owned and run by a family and its clique? That, in itself, would be a remarkable reversal of economic reality. But history is not repeating itself. A new synthesis is emerging, which combines different aspects of market capitalism and managerial capitalism, and which also transcends them in creating something quite new.

The role of the key individuals, and especially the founders, is becoming dominant in the most profitable and successful firms. This is a reversion to the nineteenth-century norm, although an early version of it. Note that even in the middle of that century, entrepreneurs became increasingly dependent on professional managers and management hierarchies. The prototype professional organization was the railroad, whose period of fastest expansion was 1840–1900. Many entrepreneurs, including Andrew Carnegie and Henry Ford, eventually lost control of their organizations.

There are many reasons that founders today are more easily able to retain their dominance, at the very time that their corporations attain their greatest value. One is that their rise (and possible fall) in value is more rapid than ever before. A second reason is that, in many cases, the capital need is much more modest. Companies based on so-called intellectual capital are more dependent on the insiders, less on external financiers. A third difference between today and the past is that companies can grow in profits and market value without continually expanding their number of employees and hence dependence on management hierarchy. This leads us to another key difference.

Today, 80/20 leaders can change an industry without having to do most of the hard work themselves, or within their corporations. They can and do outsource a majority of the activities involved in fulfilling their vision. Of course their corporations still have management hierarchies, but they are short and sweet, within the control of the top individuals. The need for management is chopped up and spread among many suppliers, so that the 80/20 leaders do not become dependent on their own management machines. When Henry Ford wanted to revolutionize the auto industry, he had to build his own corporation to do it all. Today he would simply have the idea, design and brand the car, and subcontract everything else: manufacturing, selling, distribution. By all accounts he would have been a great deal happier.

The upshot is that creative individuals are liberated from crippling dependence on capital, management, and labor. There is no longer a trade-off between continuing to grow a business and retaining personal control. 80/20 leaders can do both, and still have time for leisure, sport, art, philanthropy, or hobnobbing with the world's other rich and powerful people.

The broadly based economic rise of the individual

Today's billionaire industrial bosses are the most extreme examples of 80/20 people. Yet the rise of 80/20 people is a much longer-standing and broader process, in which creative people of all types have progressively become liberated from collective constraints.

Hollywood was a leading indicator. Hollywood studios in the 1940s were immense, broad enterprises employing writers, producers, directors, stars, cameramen, and other production staff. The corporations made the movies. They distributed them. They owned all the rights. Sometimes they also owned picture houses.

In the 1950s and 1960s, however, stars began to flex their muscles. They employed agents and lawyers to negotiate non-exclusive and shorter contracts. Producers, directors, and other individual wealth creators followed suit.

The integrated studio system has now gone. The big studios are still there, but they are mere façades. Beneath the proud brands of yesteryear, loose networks of small firms do all the work. Individuals call the shots. The big names own themselves; they keep most of the wealth they generate. In some years Steven Spielberg has earned hundreds of millions of dollars. Top actors—Tom Cruise, Harrison Ford, Tom Hanks—command over $20 million per movie. At humbler levels, other 80/20 people execute each project.

As in Hollywood, so too in sport. Time was when most profit from the industry went to TV network corporations. Then the value creators in the system staked their claims. The sports leagues were first to demand their share, but before long individual star players, such as Michael Jordan, began to negotiate for themselves.

Jordan took the process further, capitalizing on his "brand" to market products to fans. Jordan was used by Nike to endorse the Air Jordan brand of athletic shoes. Soon he forced Nike to allow him ownership of the brand.

What has happened in Hollywood and sports has also happened throughout the professions. The really juicy returns go not to corporations, nor even to partnerships, but to the few top individuals who add the most value. For instance Joseph Jamial, the world's most highly paid trial lawyer, can make $100 million in a good year.

Where the billionaires of industry, entertainment, sport, and the professions lead, a much larger number of millionaires follow. Whatever the sphere, 80/20 people can grasp control of their destiny and keep for themselves a large share of the wealth and wellbeing that they create. The secret is always to ensure that your slice of economic life revolves around you.

The transition from economic revolution to new economy

Economic revolutions are the bridge between one economy and its replacement; they are the means of transition to a new economy, not the new economy itself. As Figure 2 overleaf shows, the revolution always predates the arrival of the new economy. For example, the industrial revolution of 1750–1850 led to market capitalism, but, even in the most advanced economies, market capitalism did not dominate until the second half of the nineteenth century.

The new economy always coexists with the old economy, gradually becoming more important. At a certain stage the higher growth rate of the new economy means that it becomes a majority of the economy, but this does not happen until there have been important changes in legal rights and social conventions. At that stage, the transition to the new economy accelerates and the new economy becomes dominant, although pockets of the old economy always persist.

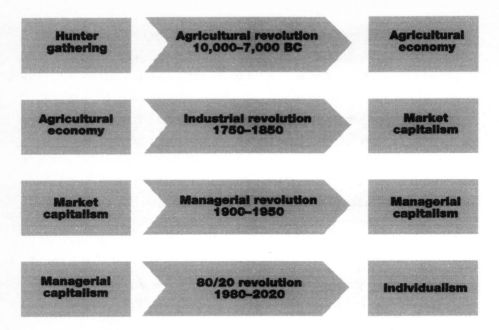

Figure 2 Revolutions: The transition to new economies

We are clearly experiencing the 80/20 revolution but not yet the new economy. The old landmarks of managerial capitalism are still intact: a corporate system that revolves more around management hierarchy than around individuals, and a stock exchange system that rewards passive investors as well as those who create new growth. Many 80/20 people, such as Rachel and her team, remain content to generate vast swathes of wealth, the great majority of which passes them by. In America and Europe there are hundred of thousands, perhaps millions, of people like Rachel.

It is probable, however, that within the next two decades, and perhaps before long, the economy will stop following the old pattern of managerial capitalism. The time will come when most corporations revolve around their key individuals, not the other way round. When this happens, the economy will change abruptly and radically. We will see a huge wealth transfer to 80/20 people, to individuals and away from institutions, to entrepreneurs and away from savers.

What would it look like, a world where capitalism is replaced by individualism, where all the Rachels get what they deserve?

Notes and references

1   Peter F Drucker (1995) *Managing in a Time of Great Change*, Butterworth-Heinemann, London. The quotation is from the superb 1994 essay, "A century of social transformations," comprising Chapter 21 of the book.

2   For an enjoyable account of hunter-gatherer society and the transition to agricultural society, see Chapter 6 of Jared Diamond (1997) *Guns, Germs and Steel: A Short History of Everybody for the Last 13,000 Years*, Chatto & Windus, London.

3   My account here owes much to collaboration with Professor Marcus Alexander, director of the Ashridge Strategic Management Centre in London. I am grateful to Marcus for permission to incorporate some of his work into this chapter.

4   Karl Marx and Friedrich Engels (1848) *The Communist Manifesto*, London. No publisher took responsibility for the 1,000 copies of the original German text printed in London.

5   Adolf A. Berle, Jr., and Gardiner C. Means (1933) *The Modern Corporation and Private Property*, Macmillan, New York.

6   Alfred D. Chandler (1977) *The Visible Hand: The Managerial Revolution in American Business*, The Belknap Press of Harvard University Press, Cambridge, MA.

7   Author's analysis based on *Fortune*, April 16, 2001, volume 143, number 8. The ownership percentages are taken from the 2001 proxy statements of Berkshire Hathaway, Microsoft, and Wal-Mart.

8   I invite a doctoral student or a consulting firm to calculate the percentage of market value accruing to individual-centered corporations over time, using different definitions. It would be particularly revealing to see a very long time series, from the start of the Dow-Jones index to today. For the most liberal definition, including companies where an executive has become a billionaire at today's values, one should of course adjust for inflation in calculating the cut-off point in each year. I also invite *Fortune* to include in its rankings an identification of individual-centered corporations, using whatever definition it considers most appropriate.

13 *What If?*

"If every person were able to capture the full value of his services, there would be no corporations."

Robert K. Elliott, vice-chairman, KPMG Peat Marwick[1]

What if... all 80/20 people get what they deserve?

The key insight from the 80/20 principle is that we always under-estimate the extent to which a few forces are super-productive. This applies to people. The Rachels of this world whip up wonderful wealth. What if they demanded their worth and enforced it, either by moving to start their own firms or by negotiating a large proportion of the profits they create?

For example, if half of the real value in the typical firm comes from creative individuals rather than the firm itself, half of the real annual surplus should, logically and equitably, go to those 80/20 people and not to shareholders.

If half of the earnings of corporate America and Europe and Japan were suddenly funneled to selected employees, the latter would clearly become very rich. But what would happen to stock markets?

Surely they would collapse. The earnings base would be halved. But shares would more than halve, because market ratings—price/earnings ratios—would be affected. The prospects for corporate earnings would suddenly dim, because the trend toward rewarding 80/20 people would not be a one-off; it would become progressively more pronounced. Companies that previously appeared to have great earnings growth prospects would now have a problematic outlook. If earnings halved, and price/earnings ratios halved, then stocks would fall by three-quarters.

Of course this won't happen, not suddenly. More likely is a slow withdrawal of 80/20 people from other people's corporations and an increase in owner-managed enterprises, things that are already evident. But however long it takes, the end result could be the same.

What if... big companies adapt to new conditions?

Under current conditions, big traditional companies—those where employees are not substantial owners—are vulnerable. If their 80/20 people leave, the growth may stop. Then the corporation would still have its existing profits, but its market rating would fall. Such firms may be rated like utilities, valued merely for their dividend yield.

But what if the more progressive big companies adapt to changed conditions? Perhaps some of them could mutate into "incubating" firms, willing hosts for new ventures started by 80/20 people. Many firms already do this, but as a sideline. What if the venturing (incubating) function—already important in many big firms, including Johnson & Johnson, Intel, and Procter & Gamble—became their main *raison d'être*?

How could this work? Imagine that one of these large corporations acquires experience and skill in attracting and nurturing 80/20 people. It would probably start by setting up its own in-house incubator, encouraging its own employees with ideas, and also 80/20 people from outside, to join the incubator.

The large corporation would enter a large number of joint ventures with 80/20 people, making its expertise and access to customers available in exchange for shares in the new entity. The corporation may acquire a reputation for helping 80/20 people set up their own business, doing so with the minimum of fuss over legal terms and the maximum interest in the new venture itself. The market for incubating corporations would probably evolve its own specialized arenas, with some incubating corporations specializing in particular industries, others in high tech, yet others in services, and others in particular geographies or in helping new ventures globalize.

Some incubating corporations would also provide capital, as GE Capital does already, while others would develop alliances with third-party venture capitalists. Some incubating corporations might even provide management, on a temporary or permanent basis, becoming expert in assessing and rounding out the management skills of entrepreneurial teams. An important part of some companies' role might be to facilitate alliances between the many new 80/20 ventures in which they have a stake.

If it is able constantly to attract new 80/20 people, and if their ventures prosper, the incubating corporation may grow its earnings indefinitely. Over time, the incubating earnings would come to dwarf the original business.

In effect, the incubating corporations could become a new type of private equity institution, but geared to the provision of industrial expertise and contacts rather than merely supplying capital.

There would be many more companies than today. Each incubating corporation may spawn hundreds of new individual-centered enterprises, each run by 80/20 people focusing on a particular, narrow sweet spot.

Alongside an increase in the number of firms, we might also see much greater variety of corporate ownership structures. As well as the conventional public listed companies there might be many private partnerships, small private firms, single-person ventures, and companies set up for specific projects—like the old East India Company—and dissolved once the project is complete.

What if... the "monetization" music stops?

Progress is never smooth and simple, or without its downsides. To date, 80/20 people have been able to benefit from the credulity of stock markets, allowing firms such as Microsoft to float on high price/earnings multiples, thus "monetizing" the value of the venture for founders and employees (see the Appendix for more details).

But what if the arguments in this book became widely accepted? What if it were seen that individuals rather than corporations or capital add value, and that any valuable corporation, even one such as Microsoft, were vulnerable to the defections of key 80/20 people?

What if the defections of people like Jeff Hawkins and Donna Dubinsky—the inventors of the PalmPilot, who fell out with the corporation that acquired them and set up Handspring, their own new venture —became commonplace rather than exceptional?

What if Microsoft investors realized more fully how dependent they are on Bill Gates and his coterie, and dumped the stock?

What if the best employees, especially newer or younger ones, demanded new and more valuable stock options, as the current ones plunge?

What if the institutional shareholders of Microsoft resisted a further transfer of wealth from them to employees?

What if the defection of the brightest young people at Microsoft caused it to lose market share?

It is not difficult to paint a picture of a downward spiral, where a yawning gap opens up between Microsoft's 80/20 people and its passive shareholders. In good times, everyone overlooks possible causes of conflict. In bad times, everyone becomes vociferous in advancing and defending their own corner.

It is not impossible to imagine Bill Gates reluctantly siding with his own people against Microsoft's institutional shareholders. In my negative scenario, he might conclude that it was impossible to shore up Microsoft's falling share price anyway, and that the best thing for his reputation and professional career would be to lead a team move of its best 80/20 people to a new corporation.

If that happened, the magic monetization music—the anomalous ability of firms dependent on a few highly talented and mobile individuals to be accorded the same high stock market rating as if they were like the previous generation of high-growth firms, where the company itself was the real source of value—would surely come to an abrupt halt.

Once stung, forever shy. Never again would investors believe that it was sensible to give an individual-centered firm a rating of 20–100 times its annual earnings, when the source of those earnings might up sticks and leave within a few years or even a few months.

Of course, my scenario of Microsoft's unraveling is very unlikely. But how implausible is it that, over the next 20 years, one high-flying new 80/20 company will see a fall-out between its 80/20 people and passive investors? How unlikely is it that one firm that investors used to believe was worth 20–100 times current earnings would suddenly become nearly worthless because of defection by its 80/20 people? One such high-profile "disaster" for investors could be all it takes to send them scuttling for cover.

What if… cash becomes king and the stock market becomes unimportant?

If 80/20 employees obtain a large minority, or a majority, of corporate profits, or if the monetization music stops, then stock markets may not only slump—they could become unimportant.

If companies' price/earnings ratios fall enough, they become attractive candidates for taking private, removing from the stock exchange. Already private buyouts are at their highest level ever, barring only the LBO explosion of the late 1980s. In 2000, for example, Seagate Technologies, the world's biggest maker of disk drives, went private in a $20 billion deal.[2]

There are many listed companies with poor growth prospects, low market ratings, but high cash flow. The stock market is not the best place for such companies to be. As Larry Shulman of The Boston Consulting

Group says, "A public corporation is a relatively risky and inefficient vehicle for accumulating cash."

A more economic alternative in a low interest rate climate is to pay off the public shareholders, reduce the equity base to a fraction of its current size, and fund the gap by debt. The cash flow can later be used to extinguish the debt. Meanwhile, the interest paid to the banks nicely reduces taxes. Even without a buyer for the company, repeated "re-capitalizations"—paying off the old debt and then loading the company with new debt—mean that cash can be taken out of the company.

Yet in this scenario it is not only low-growth companies that go private. It is also high-growth companies, which bulk much larger in the total value of the stock market. High-growth companies run by 80/20 people could become unattractive to the public market because of their dependence on the individuals. Besides increased pressure for the latter to eat into earnings previously reserved for the shareholders, there would also be the danger that the engine of profitability—the 80/20 people—could disappear without warning.

Faced with this dual pincer attack, passive shareholders might lose their nerve, sell the shares, slash the firm's market rating, and make it attractive for 80/20 people to buy back full ownership of the corporation, using debt to buy in the shares that employees don't already own.

If this happened on a big enough scale, the stock market would not merely drop like a stone; it would also rapidly become depopulated. Existing stocks would disappear while new public offerings would dry up. What investors would want would be old-style corporations they could depend on, those with growth, but not overly dependent on a few individuals. These corporations would become increasingly rare: either the firms would be low-growth and low-profit "utilities," working in the low-return areas avoided by 80/20 people, or they would be high-growth 80/20 enterprises. Neither would be desired by the stock market.

It might be that the only stocks wanted by public markets would be those offering exposure to 80/20 enterprise but in a controlled and relatively low-risk way. Examples of such stock might be old-style firms such as GE or Johnson & Johnson that had turned themselves into incubating corporations with a heavy dash of venture capital. Private equity itself would increase in importance, possibly becoming larger than public equity, although it is possible that private equity firms themselves would evolve into attractive investment vehicles on the stock market.

One side effect of any stock market decline would be a drop in the number of acquisitions of firms by other firms. These are often funded by the issue of "paper"—new shares in the acquirer—and the paper would be worth less than it used to be. But high valuations for acquired firms would also come to look increasingly suspect as those firms' earnings, and implicit price/earnings ratios, came under greater scrutiny. Why bother to acquire an asset whose value is likely to fall over time?

Venture capital and private equity evolve to back 80/20 people

As private equity and venture capital continue to expand, their character might also shift. New venture capital institutions could specialize in helping 80/20 people form joint ventures with their former employers. Some new private equity firms might tackle the opportunity from the other end, by helping large traditional firms become incubating corporations, supplying semi-captive capital to the new 80/20 enterprises. Other new venture capital houses may emerge as brokers, foraging for joint ventures between traditional firms and 80/20 people, and helping to put such deals to bed.

There might be a flowering of gentler, nicer venture houses, tailoring deals to the needs of the new teams of individuals. These houses would tout the "happiest" deals, offering 80/20 people lower leverage, lower risk, lower personal financial commitment, lower stress, and attractive but not earth-shattering returns. Compared to traditional private equity deals, the 80/20 people would have lower upside; they would make a few less millions, but be happier.

We might also see an expansion of organized and semi-organized "angel" finance. Rich individuals might band together in loose networks to back 80/20 people. Some venture capital houses may focus on providing ready-made deals for angels, taking on the burden of due diligence and financial structuring. Many 80/20 people who have already made one fortune may go on to become sponsors of a whole string of new 80/20 enterprises.

Cash becomes king

If there is increasing wariness about putting high price/earnings multiples on corporations, and if the stock market's dominance fades, we may see a change in the economy's ultimate measure of value.

This has happened before. Under feudalism, what mattered was the number of serfs or slaves, and the value and income from land. With the advent of early market capitalism, the balance sheet became the most important financial measure: the assets owned by the corporation.

In the twentieth century, the profit and loss statement became more important than the balance sheet. Earnings were king. Then, in the second half of that century, something else happened: What really mattered was not so much earnings, but the market capitalization of the company, the total market value, which was the earnings multiplied by an arbitrary number, the price/earnings ratio.

Although there were fluctuations, as the twentieth century wore on there were two clear trends: price/earnings ratios tended to rise, and also to become more volatile. The gap between earnings and market value became more pronounced, but also less reliable. Increasingly, value came to reside, or at least appeared to reside, not in today's cash, not even in today's earnings (which, again, became more and more detached from cash flows), but in the stream of earnings that it was hoped would materialize in the future.

There was always more than a touch of the emperor's new clothes about these trends. People believed in ever-escalating valuations because everybody else did. The valuations were built more and more on shifting sands. Not only were there fewer and fewer cents of earnings and assets to support each dollar of apparent value, but everyone also turned a blind eye to the evidence piling up from many quarters that increasingly the source of the earnings was mobile individuals and not the corporation and its assets.

The detachment of valuations from real cash and the real source of value is bound to end at some stage. What might the trigger for the change be?

It could be intellectual, but it could also be demographic. The stock market booms of the 1980s and 1990s coincided with the hump of baby boomers, then in their 40s and 50s, shoveling money into shares in anticipation of their retirement. Equities as a proportion of household financial assets in the US rose from 15 percent in 1985 to 34 percent in 1999. Their demand for shares raised their price and average price/earnings ratios. Whenever the stop market dipped and price/earnings ratios became more sensible, it was renewed demand from private investors, brainwashed into "buying on dips," that moved the markets back up into the stratosphere.[3]

The proportion of people in their 40s and 50s will continue to rise in the US until 2006, when it will peak at just over 40 percent of the population. It will then decline quite sharply up to 2024. During this period from 2006–24, if the retired baby boomers sell shares, particularly if they start to slip for reasons related to 80/20 enterprise, any fall in share prices could become an avalanche. The net buyers from 1985 to 2006 could be expected to become net sellers in any case, but if markets fall for non-demographic reasons there could be an unseemly rush for the exit, with baby boomers falling over each other to sell before their retirement dreams fade into a mirage.

More fundamentally, however, the effect could be to restore a sensible basis of valuation: cash instead of earnings, which are just a promise of cash in the future, and instead of market capitalizations, which represent a pyramid of hopeful expectations about earnings long into the future. Anything that calls into question the substance of those hopes may prompt an abrupt flight to cash.

Cash is the only measure understood and trusted by venture capitalists and private equity financiers. They measure their success by two benchmarks, the internal rate of return (the average compound annual return on cash) and the cash-to-cash ratio (the number of times by which any investment multiplies the cash invested). Cash is not a measure suited to the stock market. The rise of cash and of private equity, and the decline of the stock market, would be part of the same process.

Equity becomes unimportant

Even private equity could become anachronistic. For private equity houses, venture capital, and angel finance, there might be a gradual shift from owning equity—a share of permanent ownership in enterprises— to owning temporary debt instruments. Instead of owning a share of the business and hoping to make their money back several times when it is sold, venture capitalists might set a fixed annual return that could be paid back by 80/20 people at any time.

This is how it might work. I set up a new 80/20 enterprise that needs $1 million of capital. Traditionally I would give perhaps 75 percent of the ownership to a venture capitalist providing the $1 million. In the new world, the venture capitalist gets no shares but does receive the right to "interest" of 50 percent a year on the $1 million, compounded annually. The interest in the first year would be $500,000 and, if I could not pay this back, it would then be added to the principal, so that the second year's interest would be $750,000 (50 percent on $1.5m). However, as my venture generated cash I would repay the venture capitalist and have 100 percent of the company. (In practice, the venture capitalist would proba- bly own the company until he was paid back, but would have to give up his shares once repaid.)

Why would this change suit the new world? If the chance to float a company on the stock exchange dried up, and if acquisitions became difficult or unfashionable, it might be problematic to secure the "exit" that private equity houses want. They would have to get their return another way: from the cash flow of the business itself.

Another reason is that 80/20 people would be more attached to their businesses than traditional entrepreneurs; partly from choice, but partly also from necessity. If the option of getting rich quick by selling out after a few years were to fade, 80/20 people would pay increasing attention to making their business a place for their long-term careers. Without outside shareholders, it would become legitimate and socially approved to follow non-financial as well as financial criteria. Many business founders already have non-financial objectives—they want their business to endure and make progressively greater contributions to the world—but feel obliged to soft-pedal these objectives or keep them in the closet, for fear of offending financial backers. The inherent conflict between owners and executives would disappear if executives had 100 percent ownership. 80/20 people would be free to choose between financial and non-financial goals, and between short- and long-term imperatives.

If venture capitalists increasingly target a known and smooth annual return on their money, and if the success rate can be assessed statistically, then retail funds, from ordinary private investors, may be attracted to this type of investment. The venture capitalist might target a 40 percent annual return, and after losses receive 20 percent on a fairly reliable basis. The ordinary retail investor might then receive 10 percent a year, with the balance going to the individual venture capitalists. A new form of "quasi-venture capital" might gradually replace stock exchange investment, or even investment in bank deposits, for ordinary savers.

The decline of capital?

In a world of 80/20 enterprise, capital would no longer be a commodity. Its importance would decline as large and very profitable individual-centered businesses are built, like Microsoft, with little or no capital.

As capitalism fades, the rate of return on capital will continue to fall. True, there will be an explosion of new 80/20 ventures, most requiring some capital and many being able to reward their backers handsomely. On the other hand, there will be a surfeit of *emigré* capital from the public markets looking for a new home, a glut of capital chasing too few deep uses. Probably, capital will only earn high returns if it is unusually lucky or if it offers an additional ingredient—such as practical help for 80/20 enterprise.

This would mark a major change from twentieth-century experience, when passive capital, invested in the stock market, saw extraordinary returns. The most popular and reliable way to get rich in that world was to save and invest in the market. As the century closed, broad middle-class prosperity in the developed countries increasingly rested not on work but on investment in the stock market, requiring little or no skill from the savers.

Any large-scale downgrading of stock markets' size and value would have profound economic and social consequences, especially if linked to a transfer of wealth from passive investors to 80/20 people.

While sustainable wealth in the real economy would increase, the perceived wealth of most people—and indeed their real wealth, as measured by instruments such as shares—might fall rather sharply.

Effects on the economy

If any fall in the markets is a gradual process over several decades, the effect on the economy might be muted, although individual fortunes could be transformed, both ways. If stock markets crash and do not recover we could enter a serious depression, unless monetary authorities anticipate events and are able to pump liquidity into the economy.

On the other hand, a world where 80/20 enterprise is prevalent should raise employment levels, real (non-financial) market activity, and international trade and, ultimately, dampen economic swings flowing from financial speculation. We could also see a more level playing field for emerging economies, as capital becomes more available (because of its glut in the developed world) and as multinational corporations lose their ability to snap up and control successful local enterprises.

What if... partnerships become popular?

If 80/20 enterprise comprises a majority of the economy's profits, ambitious young people may start work as employees, in order to gain experience, contacts, and access to powerful ideas. But they will aim to be 80/20 people, with serious ownership where they work, by age 30. The corporate career will become a memory, if that.

More new ventures will spring up than ever before. Nearly all would be 80/20 enterprises. Before long, a majority of firms would be 80/20 ventures.

If listing on the stock exchange or selling to another corporation ceases to be the typical route for successful ventures, then most 80/20 firms may choose to become partnerships. It would be unrealistic to expect this as long as it is possible to monetize earnings through flotation or sale.

However, if these routes become unavailable there would be few advantages to 80/20 people, and many disadvantages, from having outside investors. It would be far better to have a partnership, which encourages collegiate behavior for the long term, attracting people who want to build a lengthy career, where there need be no conflict between owners and executives, and where one generation of partners benefits from the previous generation and builds for the next.

Instead of having a one-off windfall when selling or floating, 80/20 partners would become rich gradually through sharing in annual profits. With decreased capital needs, most profits may be consumed annually rather than retained.

It would also follow that the typical longevity of small enterprises would increase. This may further exaggerate the idiosyncracies of particular ventures. There would be more emphasis on the quality of working life and autonomy for individuals. There might be far greater diversity in the way that people work, and in where and when they work. Application of the 80/20 principle could reverse the current trend to longer working hours, pathological cases only excepted.

Whether or not they are partnerships, employees may generally prefer to work for 80/20 enterprises. The ethos will tend to be more personal, with less corporate bureaucracy. Typically 80/20 ventures, being more profitable and having no dividend obligations to outside shareholders, will also pay better.

What if... big becomes *passé*?

We might reasonably expect the spirit of 80/20 enterprise to overflow into the rest of society.

In the twentieth century, non-business organizations mimicked the mega-corporations. Gigantic public bureaucracies arose at city, national, and supra-national levels. Voluntary organizations followed suit, seeking to extend their size and reach. There were few objective advantages from size and many drawbacks. Still, the unspoken assumption remained: If this was the model for successful business, it must be the model for the rest of society.

However, what if the typical successful business enterprise became a medium-size partnership, owned entirely by its executives and reflecting the individual character of its founders? What lessons would the rest of society draw?

Imagine that non-business organizations re-formed around exceptional individuals, 80/20 people whose particular bent was creating wellbeing rather than wealth? Then, following the 80/20 principle, government and the social sector would radically decentralize, fragmenting into more focused units. Some of these new 80/20 social enterprises might specialize locally or by activity, while others might be entirely based around individuals, cells of creative people.

Possibly we would see the large-scale emergence of individual social entrepreneurs, 80/20 people whose mission is to increase wellbeing by using powerful ideas and working them out through a variety of joint ventures with focused non-profit entities. These 80/20 people would attract public money and private donations to achieve specific results, but contract out all work to achieve those results to existing organizations.

For example, if I wanted to end homelessness and vagrancy in Seville, I would announce my objective and the way I believed it could be achieved (for example, by personal programs for all drug addicts). I would canvass for partners, both individuals and other organizations, and for funds. If I were successful, I would encourage friends in other cities to adopt and adapt the distinctive approaches that had worked in Seville.

Successful 80/20 people would progressively attract funds, but avoid building up their own organizations.

Existing welfare and non-profit agencies would be "chopped up" into several smaller units and, as in business, become interconnected with many other entities through strategic alliances. Schools, for instance, might become more specialized, but swap teachers, students, and databases, working to improve each other's performance.

What if... individuals take charge of their destiny?

In a landscape dominated by large organizations, most people do not aspire to stamp their mark on the world. They leave their destiny to others, to organizations that already exist and that have their set patterns. They lend their lives to the past.

In a world run by 80/20 people, where business and society revolved around individuals, everyone would be challenged to take charge of their own destiny. To become an individual leader, or a partner, in creating something new and better. To affirm and celebrate the individuality inherent in every human being—to *originate* part of a richer and fuller world.

A final word on the future

My scenarios are, of course, mere illustrations of what might happen. The future cannot be safely predicted. It can only be created, by chance events as well as by the conscious efforts of millions of productive people.

The future we can enjoy depends on the quality and integrity of our dreams, on using the 80/20 principle to plug into the universe's creativity grid, and on our willingness as individuals to make the future by fulfilling our own unique potential.

The time to come will be made by 80/20 people. Why shouldn't you be one of them?

Notes and references

1 Quoted in Thomas A. Stewart (1997) *Intellectual Capital*, Nicholas Brealey, London.

2 See Larry Shulman (2000) *The End of the Public Company—As We Know It*, The Boston Consulting Group, Boston.

3 See Paul Wallace (1999) *Agequake*, Nicholas Brealey, London.

Appendix: The Roots and Ramifications of the Revolution

"Now this is not the end. It is not even the beginning of the end. But it is, perhaps, the end of the beginning."

Winston Churchill

This appendix will appeal to readers who like to relate theory and practice, and who are amenable to heresy. I lay out in more detail than in the main text the theoretical and practical roots of the 80/20 revolution, before going on to consider the radical and somewhat uncomfortable corollaries if we take the theory behind the revolution to its logical conclusion; particularly the threat to the stock exchange system that has helped to make so many of us rich.

The rise and fall of managerial capitalism

The 80/20 revolution—the process by which capitalism is beginning to be replaced by individualism—can best be understood by comparing and contrasting the rise of managerial capitalism (the economy that is still dominant, but losing ground) and the rise of individualism. Two tables summarize the changes:

Table 1 Milestones in the rise of managerial capitalism

1840s–1860s	Major construction of railroads. Railroads require management coordination and collective ownership. Invention of the managed, hierarchical, large public corporation.
1860–1900	Major technological innovation, including wireless telegraphy, the telephone, gas, electricity, and refrigeration. Technology, management, and mass production lead to large organizations. Large public-sector organizations proliferate in America and Europe: the post office, armies, navies. In Europe gas and electricity companies are typically owned by states or municipalities.
1870–1901	Andrew Carnegie reorganizes the steel industry, based on maximum scale and continuous operation of steel mills. In 1901 US Steel acquires Carnegie Steel to create a massive combine.
1905–25	Henry Ford turns the automobile industry from a fragmented market with hundreds of producers into a mass-market duopoly.
1917	Lenin seizes power in Russia and creates an organizational state, modeled on Fordist lines of industrialization, mass production, large organizations, and central management.
1900–45	Organizations acquire national scope and replace or limit markets by "insourcing" activities that used to be provided by

outside firms. Corporations become much larger in terms numbers of employees and capital employed. Market activity is reduced through industrial consolidation. International trade falls.

1933   Publication of *The Modern Corporation and Private Property*, by Adolf Berle and Gardiner Means. They celebrate "the new modern quasi-public corporation": "American industrial property, through the corporate device …[is] being thrown into a collectivist hopper wherein the individual owner is steadily being lost in the creation of a series of huge industrial oligopolies." They announce that two-thirds of American industry is controlled collectively and identify the trend toward "the separation of ownership from control."

1933–4 Hitler takes over Germany and institutes complete state direction of industry through gigantic public and private corporations.

1941   James Burnham invents the term "manager" in his influential book, *The Managerial Revolution*. "The transition from capitalist society to managerial society is already well under way."

1945–80 American (and European) multinational corporations gain unprecedented reach and economic power. The free enterprise organization proves greatly superior to the public-sector version. International trade soars.

1960–2000 The invention of the hostile takeover enables well-regarded corporations to become larger and more complex.

1970–90 The growth of diversified corporations operating in many industries.

1970–90 A few large Japanese multinational corporations achieve notable success, using highly developed central planning within each corporation.

Table 2 Milestones in the decline of managerial capitalism and the rise of individualism

---

1937–48	A series of important books celebrate individualism and warn of the dangers of collectivism to the human spirit. Particularly influential are *Anthem* (1938, 1946) and *The Fountainhead* (1943) by Ayn Rand, *The Road to Serfdom* (1944) by F. A. Hayek, and *Animal Farm* (1946) and *1984* (1949) by George Orwell.
1950–65	Hollywood stars break the studio system and capture value as individuals.
1959	Peter Drucker coins the term "knowledge workers." New knowledge-based jobs, he says, require a different mindset. Knowledge workers are self-managing and mobile.
1970–2000	Business school graduates and other ambitious individuals turn from large corporate careers to lucrative professions (accounting, consulting, investment banking, and venture capital) and starting their own enterprises. The rise and rise of venture capital and private equity provide individuals with backing for new ventures.
1975	Microsoft is founded by Bill Gates and Paul Allen. It requires minimal capital.
1975–2000	The growth of leveraged buyouts (LBOs) and buyins (LBIs) enables individuals to mutate from managers to principals. Sports and pop stars become individual enterprises. Bowie bonds issued, giving entitlement to a share of mega-star David Bowie's future earnings.
1980–2000	The star system and "winner takes all" become important in the professions generally. Large business starts to lose market share to small and medium-sized enterprise.

Companies focus on "core businesses" and sell or close the rest. Diversification becomes a dirty word—"diworsification."

1980–90   Microsoft becomes an important corporation and the proto-type for a new owner-managed enterprise: highly focused, highly profitable, highly valuable, with relatively few employees, assets or capital employed.

1986   Microsoft goes public, not to raise money but to monetize the value of employee ownership.

1990   C. K. Prahalad and Gary Hamel publish a landmark article, "The Core Competence of the Corporation," in the May–June *Harvard Business Review*. They advocate a focus on learning rather than physical assets and tell corporations to exit activities that don't use core competencies.

1990–2000 "Downsizing" and "empowerment" become all the rage. For the first time, most large organizations start progressively reducing their headcount and number of management layers. The separation of ownership from control is progressively reversed, as owner-managed enterprises become an increasing proportion of US stock market value. This trend survives the "internet bubble" of 1999–2000.
           "Outsourcing" becomes a major trend, reversing a century of insourcing and decreasing the reach and importance of management hierarchies. Strategic outsourcing—where key activities are undertaken by outside firms—becomes popular. Strategic alliances take off. The typical large corporation had zero alliances in 1989. Ten years later it had 30. Accenture estimates that alliances will represent $25 trillion of revenues by 2004.
           Academics find that by using strategic outsourcing and strategic alliances, the old trade-off between markets and corporations can be transcended. We can have both corporate planning and market efficiency, by breaking down the boundaries between organizations. Management hierarchies are less important and

orchestration across companies, without management authority, becomes crucial.

1992	Peter Drucker announces "the Fortune 500 is over." Tom Peters publishes *Liberation Management*, praising disorganization.
1993–2000	Under pressure from investors, large firms increasingly break themselves up into two or more new firms. The value of "break-ups" grows rapidly from 1993 and in 1996 exceeds $100 billion.
1996	Al Ries publishes *Focus*, showing that focused corporations are more profitable than less focused ones, and that a decade of US "unfocusing" is being corrected. Microsoft reaches a market value of $86 billion. It has less than $1 billion in net fixed assets.
1996–2000	"Virtual corporations" multiply. Whole industries become more virtual, as strategic outsourcing becomes typical.
1997	Three different books with the same title, *Intellectual Capital*, are published. A consensus emerges that brainpower is more important than physical assets and financial capital.
2000	The Boston Consulting Group says that in talent-based industries "the key unit of value creation is the *individual*" (their emphasis), not the corporation or the team.
2001	Microsoft reaches a market value of $286 billion.

A new synthesis of academic theory

Over the past decade or so, management gurus and academics appear to have gushed out a flood of fads and fancies with bewildering speed and variety. We have had core competencies, focus, downsizing, delayering, empowerment, business process reengineering, outsourcing, supply chain management, "co-opetition," strategic alliances, parenting theory, and virtual corporations. As the gurus move to carve out their own proprietary intellectual niches, they tend to stress the novel and exclusive elements of their ideas.

Yet what if these apparently competing theories are all part of one larger business trend, so that, like the blind Indian men describing an elephant, each writer has grasped one component of a larger whole? What if the common element behind all their insights is the decline of managerial capitalism and the rise of individualism? What if the common factor is the application of the 80/20 principle: the search for the most productive uses of ideas, people, capital, and everything else in the bowels of business progress?

One very useful recent academic theory explains that we can now transcend the traditional trade-off between markets and corporations. We no longer have to choose between market efficiency and corporate effectiveness. We can have both.

How? By breaking down the boundaries between one corporation and another, and between markets and corporations. Corporations can pursue strategic, long-term goals, but use markets and other organizations to fulfill them.

For example, Dell Corporation has a purpose. It aims to provide business users with a huge range of different PCs—which are permutations of different components—through direct selling, at lower cost than through traditional retail stores. A market could not organize itself to fulfill such a purpose.

In the old days, a firm such as Dell would have owned and managed a large number of assembly and subassembly operations to meet customers' needs. But Dell does not do this, and never has. What it does is to make use of a number of subcontractors who perform all of the manufacturing operations. Nor does Dell deliver its products to customers: It uses another set of subcontractors to do this. All that it does do is take orders from customers via the phone, fax, and internet, and orchestrate the process.

Why use the word "orchestrate"? Why not "manage"? To differentiate between "internal management," where managers use a hierarchy to get things done, and "external orchestration," where executives organize the process using market relationships rather than a management hierarchy.

There is a hierarchy within Dell, but it is a short one and relates only to a minority of the activity that Dell controls—the hierarchy relates to the people who take orders for computers, who are Dell's employees. But for every Dell employee, there are several other people who do what Dell wants but are employed by other firms. Dell controls a system that pursues its strategic objectives, yet more of the activity happens outside Dell than inside.

The relationship between Dell and its subcontractors is a market relationship, yet also a strategic relationship. It is not a one-off, spot market transaction. If the subcontractor performs, it may become a permanent relationship.

This system offers Dell and its customers most of the advantages of markets—efficiency and responsiveness, and the ability to weed out under-performers—with the advantages of corporations—being able to follow a strategic plan and deliberately organize the industry in a more effective and customer-pleasing way.

Most of the super-profitable new corporations that have emerged since 1975, from Nike to Microsoft to Cisco, have had this in common: they focus on a few activities, but organize a system that stretches far beyond their own corporate boundaries. They have few employees relative to their revenues and profits.

What happens inside corporations has become less important

Without our realizing it, rather a lot has happened to the corporation and its role. What used to matter was what was "inside" the corporation: its technology, know-how, factories, warehouses, sales channels, capital, and what a large number of employees, coordinated by the management hierarchy, did. The company was rich and powerful because it did things.

Now the emphasis is quite different. What matters now is what happens "between" or "outside" corporations.

Corporations used to be powerful because they bundled together a large number of different activities and attributes. They had proprietary technology. They had access to markets and to customers. Within their walls they had all kinds of experts and experienced managers. They had ideas. They had a corporate way of doing things, their own distinctive culture. They had access to special information and secrets kept from the outside world, often secrets hidden from the owners of the corporations themselves (for example, particularly profitable businesses or income streams that the managers did not want the outside world to know about). They had plenty of capital and access to any further capital that might be required. They had jealously protected brands. They owned a large number of things, including other firms.

This bundle of attributes had both elements of monopoly and elements of obfuscation. The monopoly consisted in this: If you wanted to get anything serious done in business, you needed a large corporation. Large corporations had a monopoly on the wherewithal of enterprise.

The obfuscation lay in this: The corporation was clearly valuable, since it generated increasing streams of profits; yet it was never clear what the source of the profits was. Was it the brand, or the technology, or the assets, or the customer base, or the culture, or the knowledge workers, or the managers that really generated the value? Nobody bothered to ask the question, because it didn't matter. As long as the corporation was a bundle of attributes, clearly feeding off and reinforcing each other, there was no point in trying to prioritize them. The obfuscation was related to the monopoly. If you couldn't separate out the elements of value in practice, why try to do so in theory?

The new à la carte *menu of wealth creation*

Corporations are losing their monopoly on the elements of value. These are becoming unbundled from the corporate nexus, and increasingly available *à la carte*.

Technology is more transparent and available, for example via the World Wide Web. It is becoming easier, if not always cheaper, to access other corporations' customer bases, for example through concessions in department stores, or through renting a list of customers. Ideas are also becoming liberated from corporations, carried out by individuals who leave to start a new business, cross-pollinated by the ever-burgeoning armies of consultants and information providers, or simply available on the internet. Accounting standards are being tightened, forcing corporations to reveal the true sources of their profits. Capital is available from third parties; from venture capitalists, for instance. Even high-quality brands like Virgin are on hand to outsiders, provided the terms are right.

Nobody deliberately set out to take away the corporation's monopoly on the elements of value, or to make them separately available. Few people have even noticed that this has happened. And it could never have done so, had not corporations allowed it.

Why did it occur? For greater efficiency. The economy is evolving toward more productive, transparent, and variegated ways of conducting enterprise, where the elements of value in the economy can be identified, separated, and freely traded. This is a benign process, occurring piecemeal and without any overall plan, because it raises economic returns and growth. The process is the progressive application of the 80/20 principle: "de-averaging" returns and looking everywhere for the highly productive forces, allowing value to flow freely from and to these forces.

Corporate boundaries and hierarchies become less important, individuals more important

Come back to the academic theory about markets and organizations. The professors are not saying that organizations are redundant; they are saying that the management hierarchy is less important in creating value than it used to be.

The new growth systems are created by ideas and people, and do not leverage what used to be the main rationale for corporations, the extensive management hierarchy and heavy capital requirements.

This is tremendous news for individuals. If what matters is the corporate hierarchy, tied to a bundle of corporate assets and attributes, then the individual is unimportant and dispensable. If what matters is the idea for a better economic system and the ability to orchestrate—to influence and control people who are not in your organization and over whom you have only a market sanction, not a management one—then individuals become relatively more important.

This theory fits the facts. As Wharton professor Peter Cappelli says, "It used to be that you could always walk out the door, but you couldn't do outside what you could do inside of a company. I could leave with an idea but I could never make it happen. Now, that's not the case."[2]

Value is created using the 80/20 principle

The way to generate wealth is to isolate the few most powerful and profitable forces and leverage them fully, not just at one time but continually.

Over time, each economic system (each idea, technology, product, service, individual, team, corporation, supply chain, or economy) that expands does so through superior value creation, by providing more valuable output with fewer valuable inputs.

Serious value growth happens through a never-ending stream of experiments, through new ideas that combine powerful ideas with other such ideas, through creating many variants and seeing which work best, and through taking resources from the least productive parts of every system and re-deploying them in the most productive parts.

However creative a system is, it will always have a minority of components that are several times more fecund than the others; constant improvement, therefore, is always possible.

It is the 80/20 principle that unites and describes all the practical and evident components of change that have previously been thought to be unrelated and whose significance has been under-estimated.

When corporations focus on fewer products and services, and on fewer activities, they are following the 80/20 principle. They de-average, focusing on the vital few products and activities.

When corporations outsource, they follow the 80/20 principle. They de-average.

When corporations create a new business system that involves several other corporations, but enables the innovating corporation to earn higher returns on capital, they follow the 80/20 principle. They de-average, reducing their dependence on low-return activities and increasing their focus on high-return ones.

When corporations break themselves into two or more new, separate corporations, they follow the 80/20 principle. They de-average.

When corporations confine themselves to activities using their core competencies, they follow the 80/20 principle. They de-average.

When new ventures try to identify the most profitable parts of a market and build a new business around it, they follow the 80/20 principle. They de-average, causing a smaller, more profitable business definition to emerge. The result is a greater number of smaller firms, an increase in total wealth, and a transfer of wealth from old to new firms.

When the best individuals from a firm decide to set up in business together, they follow the 80/20 principle. They are likely to demonstrate that fewer employees can generate more.

When the stars of Hollywood leave the employ of the broad-line studio corporations, they follow the 80/20 principle. They become single-person businesses for each project. Returns cannot be averaged across a large number of employees and movies. Each movie and each star becomes a separate business. Averages are blown apart.

When Michael Jordan negotiates terms for his participation on the playing field or ownership of his brand of trainers, he is following the 80/20 principle. He becomes a discrete economic unit so that he can take most of the value he personally creates.

When individuals leave Fairchild Semiconductor and start new firms, they are following the 80/20 principle. Fresh variants of old ideas, and smaller, new teams of 80/20 people, create new value.

The results of following the 80/20 principle are always the same:

❖ A new economic entity (or more than one) is created; this can be a new product segment, or a new firm, or a new project.

❖ Greater value is created for customers.

❖ There is greater selectivity than before: The previous bundle of economic activity is broken into at least two smaller bundles, enabling greater choice and a more accurate reading of preferences for each bundle.

❖ There is greater transparency between inputs and outputs: It is easier to see who and what are really producing the greatest value at the lowest relative cost.

❖ There is a closer link between value creation and value capture: The individuals and firms that create the greatest value keep a higher share of it. This encourages greater growth in the economy, by giving more resources to the most productive units, by inducing more highly productive individuals and firms to come forward, and by enabling unproductive resources to be re-deployed in more valuable ways.

The irony behind recent use of the 80/20 principle

When the 80/20 principle is taken to its logical conclusion, it undermines the classic large corporation, the typical oligarchy of the mid-twentieth century. There is a certain irony here, however, a certain rough justice.

For most of the twentieth century, the 80/20 principle was largely used by big corporations in order to attain dominant market positions. These corporations saw the logic of a few powerful forces and a mass of weaker ones as being the logic of oligopoly or even of monopoly. Firms focusing on a particular market, using the best forces available to serve that market, ended up with lower costs, more attractive brands, and higher profits, making it very difficult to overturn their dominant market positions. 20 percent of firms in a market typically ended up with more than 80 percent of it, until just two or three dominant players were left.

In 1976, Bruce Henderson wrote: "All except the two largest-share competitors will either be losers and eventually eliminated or be marginal cash traps reporting profits periodically and reinvesting forever."[3]

Until recently, it was generally accepted that the 80/20 principle would favor corporate size and industrial concentration. Yet now it turns out that there is more to competition and definition of business systems than was ever dreamt about in the past. Competition need not be, and increasingly is not, confined to the overall level of activity in the market as a whole. Both activity and the market can be split into many layers and niches.

Are organizations deconstructing?

Philip Evans and Thomas S. Wurster of The Boston Consulting Group go further. They herald "the deconstruction of the organization":

> *"Decentralized self-organization—the ability of employees to group together, break apart, and regroup across corporate boundaries—will flourish as small companies … collaborate with each other. As enterprises learn to do this, they will demonstrate the ability to complete complex projects that had previously been possible only through the hierarchical direction of the large corporations.*
>
> *"The ultimate challenge posed by deconstructing supply chains will be to the organization itself. If multiple, smaller organizations can self-organize and collaborate through a pattern of fluid alliances, this raises an interesting question as to why, precisely, the large hierarchical corporation is needed at all."[2]*

Consider the case of Linus Torvalds, a Finnish software designer. In 1991 he invented an operating system and named it Linux. He put it out on the web, freely available, and invited the IT-heads of the world to debug the system. Linux was developed without capital and, initially, without a corporation. In desktop computers it is miles behind Windows, but by

2000 Linux had taken 31 percent of the web server market. It is Microsoft's major rival.

Microsoft vice-president Paul Maritz put it this way in 1999: "It's almost as though the village blacksmiths of the world can now build axles in their back yard and assemble them together and compete with General Motors. And that's literally what is going on. We have proof through the Linux operating system."[4]

Both Linus Torvalds and Bill Gates are 80/20 people. Both have created enormous new value. Neither needed third-party capital. One used a corporation; one didn't. In neither case was the corporation the source of value. Microsoft is just the vehicle used by Bill Gates and his small team to capture the value that they have created as 80/20 individuals.

The importance of individuals challenges the shareholder theory of the firm

What made the corporation valuable to passive outside shareholders was its machine-like characteristics. What made the outside shareholders valuable to the corporation was that building a large, integrated corporation and a large management hierarchy required lots of capital. To insiders and outsiders alike, the corporation was a machine, a black box. In went capital and out came profits. If the machine produced stable profits it was worth a few years' earnings. If the machine produced growing profits it might be worth 20, 30, or even 50 times earnings.

However, what if the corporation is not a machine? What if it depends on a few individuals? Specifically, what if the growth, which is what really makes corporations valuable, depends more on individuals and ideas, which the individuals generate or can appropriate, than it does on the corporate machine? What if Bill Gates is right when he says "Take away our 20 most important people, and I tell you we would become an unimportant company."

Then the shareholder theory cannot cope. If 80/20 people are more important than capital, a majority of the annual distribution of profits should go to these individuals and not to stockholders. Even more importantly, it makes no sense to value the corporation at a high multiple of profits, if the individuals behind the profits can leave and take the growth prospects of the corporation with them.

We saw earlier the saga of the two 80/20 leaders of PalmPilot and how they ran rings around the corporation that acquired them, setting up a new corporation, Handspring, with the right to license the Palm technology. Similar stories abound. To take two at random, IBM spent $3.5 billion to acquire Lotus Development Corporation, "but more importantly," an analyst wrote, "its chief programmer." I wish IBM luck. At the same time the *Boston Globe* reported that Lucent spent some $900 million buying Nexabit Networks in June 2000, only to see its founder leave within a year, leading several key employees to a new venture opened literally across the street.

If intellectual capital is really more important than the "real" capital frozen in the corporate machine, the "real" capitalists are up a gum tree. One might conclude that, in the search for efficiency and effectiveness, corporations have dug their own graves and those of their financial backers.

If corporations don't do what 80/20 people want, the latter can leave and start their own firms. For good ideas and good people, capital will be forthcoming. 80/20 people may also be able to ally with the corporations of their choice. What is good for the individual established corporation— an expansion of its profits through alliance with a startup run by a small team of individuals—may sound the death-knell of established corporations as a whole.

The illogical theory behind today's stock market

The shareholder theory of the firm is that firms go to stock exchanges for capital, and that is why passive shareholders should be rewarded with dividends and other ownership rights.

However, Microsoft did not need capital. Founded in 1975 and incorporated in 1981, Microsoft only went to the stock exchange in 1986.

With commendable frankness, Microsoft's Michael Brown explains why:

> *"For pure information age companies ... when these companies go public,*
> *they don't do it to raise proceeds to build plants. They do it to monetize the*
> *value of their employee ownership schemes. Microsoft was originally incor-*
> *porated to create a vehicle to share ownership ... And the principal reason*
> *we went public was to monetize the value."*[5]

"Monetize the value" is a wonderful expression. Put more bluntly, it means that Microsoft listed in order to make Bill Gates and his partners billionaires, and some less exceptional (or later) employees millionaires. More precisely, the reason was to capitalize these 80/20 people's earnings, to place a very high multiple on the value of each year's profits. If Microsoft had been arranged as a partnership, Bill and his chums might still have become billionaires, but they would be poor billionaires, 20 or 30 times poorer than they are.

Perhaps I should not be saying this, but if you stop to think about it, "monetizing the value" of companies is a very odd reason to have a stock market. The reasoning is circular, and works in practice but not at all in theory.

Some 80/20 people, like Gates & Co., start a firm. They want to maximize their wealth. They are good at what they do, latch on to powerful business genes, create their own unique variants of new ideas, demonstrate a continual ability to reach the second, third, and subsequent stages of growth by producing yet new variants of success, and create great wealth.

Although some of this wealth is built into the corporate machine, a majority of the wealth-creating ability still emanates from the top individuals in the company. They list on the stock market not because this is the only way to get capital, but because this is the best way for them to maximize their wealth. If they had not listed, even if they had kept all the profits themselves and not "given some away" to capital, they would not be so rich.

The system works, but only because it directly contradicts the traditional theory of the quoted company. The old theory—which fitted the old practice—was that capital was more important than labor. Because a great deal of capital was needed, the capitalists took the vast majority of the equity in the company and those who ran the company took little or none. The firm belonged to the owners and the managers were dispensable hired hands.

In the new practice, the firms do not require a great deal of capital and are potentially extremely profitable. Therefore, the founders are able to retain a large slug of the equity.

Because they have a large share, and because the public markets will multiply annual profits by a large number to arrive at the value of the firm, the founders want the shares to be quoted. They are motivated by the stock market value of the firm. They want to monetize the value.

If you told 80/20 people that they could keep all the profits of the firm each year but that their shares had no other value, they would refuse that deal. 80/20 people prefer to have a lower share of the company and allow capital a share, if it means that the company can be quoted and have a higher value.

The practice only works because the capital need is modest relative to the value of the corporation. If Bill Gates had a very small share in Microsoft, he would do better to take his top 20 people and start another firm. The value of Microsoft is supported because the stock market knows that he has a large share and will act to protect it. If Microsoft had needed the sort of capital that highly valuable companies used to require, Mr. Gates could not have had such a large share, the stock market would know that he and his best people might leave, and the company could never have become so valuable.

Conclusion

One has to ask: Why have a stock market system if it serves no other economic function than to make 80/20 people rich? I like the result, but the logic behind it eludes me.

If the stock market did not exist and capital was relatively unimportant compared to individuals, no one could possibly dream up such a system and be taken seriously. It would have all the credibility of a chain letter scam.

That is why, ultimately, I am convinced that our economic system will change. As some 80/20 people demand a higher share of today's corporate earnings and other 80/20 people leave to found their own enterprises, "shareholder value" based on the classic corporation where ownership and management are separated will work neither in theory nor practice. Those individuals who generate the wealth will find ways to keep most of it, although increasingly in the form of annual distributions of profits rather than in get-rich-quick deals on the stock market. The providers of capital will have to master some other skill, or strike a bargain with individuals who have other skills, to ensure that they select the few investments that will yield high returns to capital after the claims of the individual wealth creators have been met.

There is both justice and market efficiency in the notion of economic individualism. Peter Ustinov quipped that "under capitalism certain people are exploited by other people, whereas under communism it is just the other way round." Under individualism, nobody will be exploited but everyone will have to exploit their own abilities to the full.

In the long run more wealth will be created, as we remove market imperfections blocking the natural flow of wealth to its creators. Yet revolutions are never easy, and the short- to medium-term ride brought by the 80/20 revolution may be bumpy in the extreme. It will be up to each of us as individuals and teams of individuals to ensure that we are on history's winning side.

Notes and references

1   Quoted in *Wharton Alumni Magazine*, Winter 2000, p. 10.
2   Bruce Henderson quoted in Carl W. Stern and George Stalk Jr. (1998) *Perspectives on Strategy*, John Wiley, New York.
3   Philip Evans and Thomas S. Wurster (2000) *Blown to Bits*, Harvard Business School Press, Boston.
4   *United States of America versus Microsoft Corporation et alia*, Washington DC, January 26, 1999, pp. 60–61.

5   Quoted in Thomas A. Stewart (1997) *Intellectual Capital*, Nicholas Brealey, London, p. 105.

Index

3Com 126–7
16 times rule 97–9
20 percent spike 36, 44–8, 52, 85, 94
80/20 billionaire 26–7, 192, 196–7
80/20 parsimony principle 152
80/20 people 4, 8–9, 12
    and capital 157–70
    and other firms 141–55
    and their firms 117–39
    and over-production 143–5
    colorful CEOs 192
    corporations revolve around 192–6
    enlisting 97–115
    illustration of value of 139
    not taking value they create 198
    potential rewards to 200–14
    rise of 14–30
80/20 principle 3–7
    and big business 27
    and creation 9–12
    and de-averaging 71, 132, 227–9
    and the hamburger 47
    and new business 28
    dynamics of 173–4
    empirical law and examples 99
    irony behind recent use 229–30
    value created by 227–9
80/20 revolution 3–4, 7, 190–8
    key elements reversing managerial
    revolution 190–1
    new way of creating wealth 4–5,
    191–2

80/20 rule 6
    see also 80/20 principle

Accenture 22
agricultural (feudal) economy 198
agricultural revolution (10,000–7,000 BC)
    11, 185, 198
agricultural revolution (1750–1850 AD)
    11
Alexander, Professor Marcus 199, 243
Allen, Paul 220
Allin, Mark 135
Amazon.com 192
American Civil War 187
American Revolution 187
angel finance 166–7, 206–7
"Anton" 113
AOL Time Warner 193
Archimedes 14
AT&T 187–8
averages 19, 71
    see also de-averaging

Bain & Company 54–5, 134
Bain, Bill 54, 77, 110, 123
Bain Capital 79
Bains, Gurnek 36
Bartlett, Christopher A. 139
Beinhocker, Eric D. 156
Belgo 90–2, 94–5, 179–80
bell curve 99–100
Benhamou, Eric 126

Berkshire Hathaway 192–3
Berle, Adolf, and Gardiner Means
    187–8, 193, 199, 219
Betfair 60–1, 90
Bezos, Jeff 15, 36, 192
big becomes passé 213–14
Bill, story of 147–8
    see also Gates, Bill
Birt, Sir John 44
"Bjorn-Ingvar" 41–2
Black, Andrew 60
Black Entertainment Television 26, 30
Blais, Denis 94
BMW motorcycles 78
Boscariot, Olivo 42–3
Boston Consulting Group, The (BCG)
    48, 53–4, 92, 122–6, 134, 222
boundaries of the corporation 224–7
Bower, Marvin 52, 58, 64, 123–4
Bowie, David 15, 220
Bowskill, Jerry 118–19, 127–8
Branson, Richard 15, 192
breakups 222
Brown, Michael 233
Buffett, Warren 15, 21, 192–3
Burnham, James 219
Burton, Richard 135–6
Bush, George W. 15
business genes 48–9, 101–3

capital 157–70
    decline of 210–12
    declining rate of return 191–2
    less of a barrier to 80/20 people
        159–63
    no longer the driver of growth
        161–3, 233–5
capitalism 161
    managerial capitalism, rise of 188–90
    managerial capitalism, decline of
        190–2,
    market capitalism 197–8
    replacement by individualism

        184–98, 200–14, 217–35
cash
    obsession with 169
    becomes king 204–11
    ultimate measure of value 207
cash-to-cash ratio 163–5
Capstone Publishing 135, 181
Carnegie, Andrew 17, 193, 195, 218
Caven, Niall 57, 94
Champy, James 46
Chandler, Alfred D. 181, 199
Chrysler 27, 176
Churchill, Winston 2, 217
Cisco 224
Clark, Jim 15
Coca-Cola Corporation 194
Colombo, Christoforo 15, 17, 157–9
Collischon, David 178
communism 235
core competence, competencies 221
corporate venturing 201–2
corporations
    and managerial capitalism 187–90
    and over-production 141, 143–5
    decline of managerial capitalism
        190–2
    less important than individuals 4,
        184
    monopoly of means of production
        189
    monopoly ends 190–1
    new breed of 192–6
Cruise, Tom 196
cuckoo, how to be one 145–7

Dalton, James 181
Darwin, Charles 17, 18, 48, 62–3, 116,
    174
Davies, Norman 171
Dawkins, Richard 48, 62, 64
de-averaging 71, 132, 226–9
deconstruction 230–1
Dell Computer Corporation 81, 223–4

demographic shifts 208
Diamond, Jared 199
Domino's Pizza 79
downsizing 221
Drucker, Peter F. 184, 199, 220, 222
Dubinsky, Donna 126–7, 203

East India Company 202
Ecclesiastes 12
Edge, Gordon 135
Einstein, Albert 17–18, 85, 86–96, 103
Elliott, Robert K. 200
Ellison, Larry 192
    see also Oracle
equity
    becomes unimportant 209–11
Evans, Iain 48, 108,
Evans, Philip 2, 31, 230, 235
evolutionary psychology 111

Fairchild Semiconductor 228
feudalism 198, 207
Field, Robin 49, 73, 85, 178, 244
Filofax 73, 177–9
"fleas and elephants" 23–4
Flintstones, the, and the docile
    brontosaurus 142
Ford, Gerald 15
Ford, Harrison 196
Ford, Henry 15, 17, 51, 176–7, 193, 195,
    218
Ford Motor Corporation 27, 176–7
Formule 1 80
Forster, E. M. 172
Fortune 50 companies 20, 149
Fortune 20 companies 193–4
Fuller, Thomas 61

Gajilan, Aryln Tobias 139
Gates, Bill 2, 15, 17, 21, 25, 27, 36, 192,
    203, 220, 231–4
GE (General Electric) 194, 205
GE Capital 202

General Motors 2, 26–7, 176, 231
Generics Group, The 135
Ghoshal, Sumantra 139
Gladwell, Malcolm 31
Goizueta, Robert 194
Goldman Sachs 26, 122, 192,
Gore, Al 15
Grantovetter, M. 156
Greenspan, Alan 162
Grisham, John 15
Grove, Andy 15, 36, 117, 192

Haller, Rick 119–20, 127–8, 132–4
Hamel, Gary 221
Handspring 126–7, 232
Handy, Charles 23
Hanks, Tom 15, 196
Harris, Philip 2
Hawkins Jeff 126–7, 203
Hayek, F.A. 150, 156, 220
Henderson, Bruce D. 53–4, 58, 110,
    122, 124, 235
Hewlett-Packard 20, 192
hierarchy 188–90, 198
    decline of management hierarchy
    190–1, 213–14, 220–35
    growth of management hierarchy
    187–9, 218–19
    monopoly of means of production
    225
Hitler, Adolf 219
Hollywood 196–7, 228
Honda 78
Hounshell, David 50, 64
Hugo, Victor 45
hybrid solutions 132–3, 139

IBM 6, 26, 156, 232
incubators 118–19, 201–2
individual-centered corporations 192–6,
    198
individualism, new economic system of
    184–98, 200–14, 217–35

individual, rise of 14–30, 192–8,
  199–214, 217–35
"individualized corporation" 133,
  139–40
internal rate of return (IRR) 163–5
Ikea 80
industrial revolution 4, 186–7, 197–8
insourcing, internalization of market
  activity 189–90, 218–19
Intel 28, 201
intellectual capital 24–5, 30, 222, 232

Jackson, Michael 100
Jamial, Joseph 197
Jefferson, Thomas 2
Jobs, Steve 36, 192
Johnson & Johnson 201, 205
Johnson, Robert 15, 30
Jones, Barry 125–8, 132–4
Jordan, Michael 15, 100, 196–7, 228
Judge's gambit 168–9
Judge, Sir Paul 130–2, 168–70
Juran, Joseph Moses 6, 12

Keynes, John Maynard 16–17
Kim, W. Chan 85
Kinepolis 80–1
Kiuchi, Tachi 13
Koch's law of individual wealth creation
  99–101

Laurie, Don 30, 156
Lawrence, Jim 48, 108
LBO explosion 204, 220
LEK 54–6, 82, 108, 111, 123, 149, 177
Lenin, V. I. 218
Lexus 79
Lifepi 49
Linux 2, 6, 230–1
Lotus 6, 232
Lucent 232

Maccoby, Michael 36, 49

managerial capitalism, managerial
  revolution 4, 187–90, 198
  retreat of 190–2, 220–35
  rise of 218–19
Mandela, Nelson 15
Maritz, Paul 2, 231
Mars, John and Forrest 193
Marx, Karl 141, 155, 186, 199
Matsushita, Konosuke 17
Mauborgne, Renée 85
McKinsey 48, 52–3, 123–4
McLuhan, Marshall 86
Microsoft 2, 6, 20–1, 25, 28, 82, 147,
  192–3, 203–4, 210, 220–4, 231–4
Milgrom, P.R. 156
Mill, John Stuart 22
missing markets 150
Model T Ford 50
Morita, Akio 17
Mother Teresa 15

NEC 78
Newton, Sir Isaac 15, 17, 18, 97
Nexabit Networks 232
Nike 82, 197, 224
Nightingale, Florence 15

oddballs, value of 110
Oracle 26, 192
orchestration 224
Orwell, George 15, 220
outsourcing 221
over-production 141, 143–5
ownership and control
  separation of 187–9
  reunited 190

PA Consulting 135, 149
PalmPilot 126–7, 203, 232
Pareto principle, Pareto rule 99
  see also 80/20 principle
Pareto, Vilfredo 4–6, 85, 116, 244
partnerships 122–6, 128, 134, 211–12

Pennsylvanian Railroad 187
Plisnier, André 94
Plymouth Gin 145–8, 150, 153, 181
Prahalad, C. K. 221
Premier Brands 131, 168–9
PricewaterhouseCoopers (PwC) 119
private equity, evolution of 206–7
Procter & Gamble 201
productive narcissists 36

Queen Elizabeth II of Great Britain 15

"Rachel" 38–40, 61–2, 82–3, 95,
    114–15, 132, 136–8, 148, 198, 243
Rand, Ayn 220
Reagan, Ronald 15
Reeve, Jamie 43, 113–14
"Richard" 120–1
Ries, Al 222
Rockefeller, John D. 193
Rocking Frog 118–19, 128
Roddick, Anita 192
Russian computer algorithms 171
Rutherford, Professor Ernest 157

Schumpeter, Joseph 63, 161, 171
Seagate Technologies 204
second stage of growth 172–81
self, yourself 35
Shakespeare, William 35
shareholder theory 231–4
Shaw, George Bernard 38
Shulman, Larry 141, 155–6, 204, 215
Skidelsky, Robert 30
Sonley, Nick 57, 94
Sorensen, Charles 51, 64
Soros, George 192
Southwest Airlines 80
sports industry 196
Spielberg, Steven 15
star system 220
strategic alliances 221
Steindl, Josef 99, 116

Stewart, Thomas A. 30, 215, 236
stock exchange system 198
    vulnerability of 201, 204–11, 217–35
superstar CEOs 36, 192

Thurow, Lester C. 116, 162, 171
time relativity, time revolution 86–95
tipping point 28–9
Tom and Jerry 142
Torvalds, Linus 230–1
Toyota 27, 79

US Post Office 187
US Robotics 126

value, measures of 207–11
Vautier, Geoffrey R. 116
Vin & Sprit 146, 153
Virgin 192

young talent 105–7

Wallace, Paul 215
Walton, Sam 15, 17, 174–5, 181, 193
Wal-Mart 174–5, 192–3
wealth creation multiple 100–1
    see also business genes
wealth/talent arbitrage, theory of 104–5
wealth transfer, coming 198
Welch, Jack 36, 194
Winfrey, Oprah 12, 192
winners and sex 176
winner takes all 220
Winnett, Robert 49
Wolf, Martin 116
Wray, Edward 60
Wurster, Thomas S. 2, 31, 230, 235

Yudelowitz, Jonathan 49

Zoffany Hotels 57, 61, 94, 142, 150–1,
    180

Acknowledgments

The 80/20 Revolution grew out of a project to combine Dr. Marcus Alexander's insights on the "boundaries of the corporation" with my own ideas from work on *The 80/20 Principle* and other books. Marcus is a director of the Ashridge Strategic Management Centre based in London, and his intellect and intuition were invaluable in stimulating my thinking, particularly relating to Part III. The ideas in Chapter 12 evolved directly from our collaboration. I owe a huge debt to Marcus and cannot thank him enough. Having said that, I have probably gone much further in my conclusions than he would have done, and of course all errors of fact and interpretation are entirely mine.

My second terrific debt is to "Rachel," a colleague and friend. She is flesh and blood, alive and well, disguised only to protect the guilty. All her associates will know who she is, and I am profoundly thankful for Rachel's willingness to bare her soul in print. May she go on to the full riches she deserves.

Next I must pay tribute to all the individuals whose stories are told in the book, especially those who are still living and who gave their permission for inclusion. I do not mean that I have been bumping off the recalcitrant individuals, just that some are historical figures or already well known.

I very much appreciate the assistance given in shaping the book by Nicholas Brealey, Sally Lansdell, and Sue Coll, all of whom have made major contributions and greatly improved the book's flow, and the aid from my "usual suspects" of readers, advisers, and supporters. Particular credit goes to my friends Aaron Calder, Chris Eyles, Robin Field, Matthew Grimsdale, Juliet and Peter Johnson, and Patrick Weaver.

Finally, praise be to the great Vilfredo Pareto, who set the ball rolling in the first place.

Visit the 80/20 website

www.the8020principle.com

The 80/20 principle is a truly global concept that applies to the whole range of life experiences—our personal and work lives, and our physical, economic and social environments.

The 80/20 website (www.the8020principle.com) is a global resource for "things 80/20," where you have free access to summaries of *The 80/20 Principle* and *The 80/20 Revolution* and can exchange views and stories about the impact of 80/20 on your life and work.

The site provides:

A structured link to 80/20 material on the web:

Infomercials, articles, case studies, checklists, handy charts, marketing tips, telling stories, software products and much, much more!

For instance, how can the 80/20 principle save billions of dollars in procurement, find winners in the UK racing industry, or point you to the best spots to fish?

A market space to exchange commercial products and services that apply the 80/20 principle, including:

consultants, professional speakers, training courses, time management techniques, books and CDs.

A forum for 80/20 ideas:

Have your say, contact with the experts, and bring your own case studies so we can all learn.

Visit www.the8020principle.com today and spread the secret of achieving more with less